Practicing for STAAR Success

Grade **4** Mathematics

Author
Beth Mundy

Publishing Credits

Corinne Burton, M.A.Ed., *President*; Conni Medina, M.A.Ed., *Managing Editor*; Emily R. Smith, M.A.Ed, , *Content Director*; Aubrie Nielsen, M.S.Ed., *Content Director*; Kat Bernardo, M.Ed., *Editor*; Reha Jain, M.Ed., *Editor*; Courtney Patterson, *Multimedia Designer*; Don Tran, *Graphic Designer*; Tara Hurley, *Assistant Editor*

Image Credits

Noted graphics and visuals provided by *TIME For Kids*. *TIME For Kids* and the *TIME For Kids* logo are registered trademarks of TIME Inc.

All other images are from Shutterstock.com, unless otherwise noted.

Standards

Shell Education

a division of Teacher Created Materials
5301 Oceanus Drive
Huntington Beach, CA 92649-1030
ISBN 978-1-4258-1703-9
https://www.tcmpub.com/shell-education
© 2017 Shell Educational Publishing, Inc.

Table of Contents

Today's Tests

Most teachers enter the field of education because they have a passion for learning and hope to share that with students. Parents hope their children spend the hours in their classrooms engaged in lessons and activities that foster that love of learning. Few stakeholders in education have a passion for standardized testing or practicing for those tests. However, such high-stakes testing is a reality.

Scales, scores, and assessments are absolutely necessary to ascertain the academic progress of students. This kind of data is vital for teachers to evaluate student achievement and determine next steps for instruction. As standards have become more rigorous, assessments that measure progress require the higher-level thinking skills necessary to prepare students for college and careers.

Students and teachers need high-quality resources that present students with more rigorous questions that will prepare them for today's tests. *TIME For Kids: Practicing for STAAR Success* incorporates the expectations of the Texas Essential Knowledge and Skills (TEKS) and focuses on the content tested on the State of Texas Assessment of Academic Readiness (STAAR) assessments.

The following pages serve to explain the format of the STAAR program, which was developed and adopted by the Texas School Board of Education, and replaced the previously administered Texas Assessment of Knowledge and Skills (TAKS). Tips for making testing practice meaningful and effective are also included to guide teachers and parents in the use of this resource. Question types that reflect those found on the STAAR tests provide authentic practice opportunities for students.

With the efficient and purposeful testing practice offered in *TIME For Kids: Practicing for STAAR Success*, students can feel prepared to demonstrate their knowledge on the STAAR test, and educators can confidently focus on developing the love of learning that keeps students on the path to achievement.

Today's Tests *(cont.)*

The State of Texas Assessment of Academic Readiness (STAAR) Program

The STAAR program was implemented in 2012 by the Texas Education Agency (TEA) to assess the Texas Essential Knowledge and Skills (TEKS). These assessments focus on Readiness for college and/or careers with test questions that focus on rigor and critical analysis.

At the elementary and middle school levels, the Mathematics TEKS are assessed with STAAR Mathematics. STAAR Mathematics is given to students each year in grades 3–8. STAAR Spanish Mathematics is offered in grades 3–5. Additional tests within the STAAR program include the STAAR L, a language-modified assessment for eligible English language learners, and STAAR A, an online version with embedded accommodations for students with disabilities (Texas Education Agency 2014).

The general STAAR and STAAR Spanish are available on paper only. Students must complete the assessment within four hours, unless students meet the criteria for accommodations of extra time. The question format is primarily multiple-choice, and students record their answers on an answer sheet. In addition to the multiple-choice questions, there are three "griddable items" on each STAAR Mathematics test in grades 3–5. These questions are open-ended, and require students to bubble in a numeric answer (Texas Education Agency 2014).

Grade 3 Mathematics   Grades 4–5 Mathematics

Students' scores on STAAR are reported as one of three categories:

- Level III: Advanced Academic Performance

- Level II: Satisfactory Academic Performance

- Level I: Unsatisfactory Academic Performance

Level II is considered the passing standard on STAAR, so students scoring at Level II or Level III have passed, while students scoring at Level 1 have not passed.

Today's Tests (cont.)

The State of Texas Assessment of Academic Readiness (STAAR) Program (cont.)

Reporting Categories for STAAR Mathematics

The Texas Education Agency has identified certain TEKS that are eligible for assessment on STAAR Mathematics and have defined four reporting categories for those standards: *Numerical Representations and Relationships*, *Computations and Algebraic Relationships*, *Geometry and Measurement*, and *Data Analysis and Personal Financial Literacy*. The mathematical process standards are incorporated into the assessment within the four reporting categories. A brief description of the reporting categories is provided below. For a complete list of the TEKS evaluated in each reporting category, visit the TEA website at www.tea.texas.gov.

Reporting Category 1: Numerical Representations and Relationships

Reporting Category 1 assesses students' ability to work with numbers and expressions. The Number and Operations standards around the base-10 place value system and fractions are addressed in this reporting category.

Reporting Category 2: Computation and Algebraic Relationships

The questions in Reporting Category 2 assess how well students perform operations and model algebraic relationships. *The Number and Operations* and *Algebraic Reasoning* standards addressing fluency, problem solving, and algorithms are assessed in Reporting Category 2.

Reporting Category 3: Geometry and Measurement

Reporting Category 3 poses questions that assess students' understanding of geometry and measurement. All of the grade-level eligible TEKS for the Geometry and Measurement standards are assessed in this reporting category, along with Algebraic Reasoning standards related to perimeter and area.

Reporting Category 4: Data Analysis and Personal Financial Literacy

Reporting Category 4 presents questions that require students to analyze data and demonstrate an understanding of personal financial literacy. All of the grade-level eligible TEKS for the Data Analysis and Personal Financial Literacy standards are assessed in this reporting category, along with Number and Operations standards associated with money.

Readiness Standards versus Supporting Standards

In the process of developing the STAAR Program, the TEA made a distinction between "Readiness" and "Supporting" standards that are eligible for assessment. Those standards that have been designated as "Readiness" are considered the most crucial for success with the curriculum, and have a heavier focus in STAAR tests. While the "Supporting" standards are deemed important for instruction, they may or may not be tested each year.

How to Use This Resource

The practice exercises in this resource have been designed to offer students the opportunity to prepare for STAAR Mathematics by providing questions aligned to the eligible TEKS, in a style and format that mirrors STAAR tests.

In order to succeed on STAAR, students must be able to correctly record answers on a separate answer sheet. While the practice exercises in this book can certainly be used without the answer sheet, including its use as part of test preparation gives students practice with properly filling in bubbles and finding the correct location to record an answer for each test item.

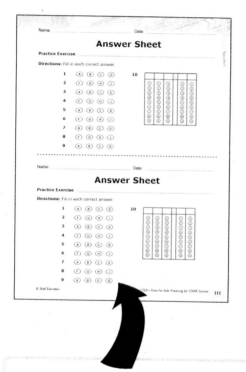

Make copies of the answer sheet and cut them in half on the dotted line. Have students use a half-sheet to record their answers for each practice exercise.

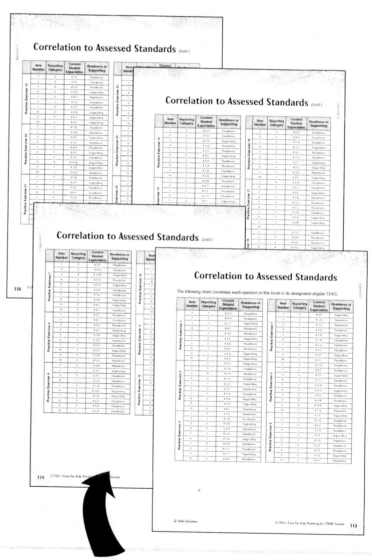

The Correlation to Assessed Standards chart on pages 113–116 provides information on the reporting category, standard, and type of standard (Readiness or Supporting) for each test item.

Making It Meaningful

This section has been included to make this book's test practice more meaningful. The purpose of this section is to provide sample guiding questions framed around a specific practice exercise. This will serve as a meaningful and real-life application of test practice. Each guiding question focuses on strands of mathematics as well as test-taking strategies. The making-it-meaningful questions may be used with students as a teacher-led think aloud or to individually assess how students are approaching and understanding complex mathematical ideas and concepts. The framework used in this model serves as a template for how to approach all the practice exercises in this product. This template supports educators in preparing students for today's tests and helps make meaning of mathematical standards used in classrooms today.

When multiple choice questions have only one correct response, guide students in the following way:

"After reading the problem, can you use logical reasoning to eliminate any responses that do not make sense? How do you know they cannot be correct? Cross them out. Finally, reread and solve the problem, and select the best answer."

When students encounter multiple-choice questions with more than one correct solution, coach them to practice the following approach:

"Examine all your options. Make a convincing argument as to why each one is true or not true."

For all open-ended problems, students should ask themselves the following questions:

"Could I explain this problem to someone else? Do I have to ask any questions to understand the problem better? What is my plan to solve this problem? How can I model my thinking? Is my plan working, or do I need to make adjustments? Does my solution make sense?"

Making It Meaningful (cont.)

When problems include specific math vocabulary terms, help students in the following way:

"What math terms appear in the problem? Circle them. How can understanding the meanings of the terms help you solve the problem?"

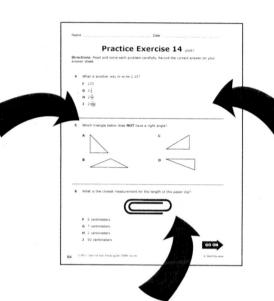

Math problems often include models. Guide students in the following way to encourage active use of problem-solving strategies:

"What can you tell us about the model? Have you seen this model, or something very similar, during previous learning? How can using what you know about the model help you solve the problem?"

Estimation can help determine the reasonableness of a solution or can be a solution itself. Provide support in the following way:

"Is an estimate an appropriate solution or is an exact solution also required? Are there rounded numbers you could use to formulate your estimate? What is your best option for estimating? Should you round to the nearest half? Should you round to the nearest whole number? Or should you round to a certain place value?"

Having multiple-choice answers for a problem can be a teaching opportunity for using logical reasoning. Coach students to try the following approaches:

"After reading the problem and its choices, guess and check to see which solution is correct. Or try working backward from each answer to see if it makes sense for the problem."

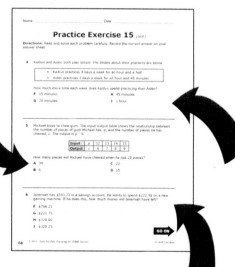

When examining a table, chart, or graph, use guiding questions to help students organize their thinking and activate background knowledge:

"What type of table, chart, or graph is this? What questions can you answer based on the information given?"

When selecting an operation to solve a problem, prompt students:

"Reread the problem. What important words appear to help you choose the correct operation and make a plan to solve?"

Making It Meaningful *(cont.)*

When a problem includes challenging numbers, provide support in the following way:

"Can you create a simpler problem? How can solving the simpler problem help you make a plan for the original problem? Can the simpler problem give you any information about the actual solution?"

If students need to complete a table, chart, or graph, support them with the following guiding questions:

"What type of table, chart, or graph do you need to make? What information will it show? Do any components already appear? Which components do you need to add or include? Do you need to add any labels or titles to make your work complete and understandable to others?"

When solving problems with data from multiple sources, students should ask themselves:

"What information do I need to gather? Where can I find the needed information? Is there any data given that I do not need to answer the question? How can I organize my thinking and data to make a plan and solve the problem?"

To support students in preparing for today's tests, send home the *Top Tips: Preparing for Today's Tests* on page 117. This page is intended to guide parents at home in how to prepare their children for tests. Page 118 gives students a list of strategies they can use at school to be more successful while taking tests.

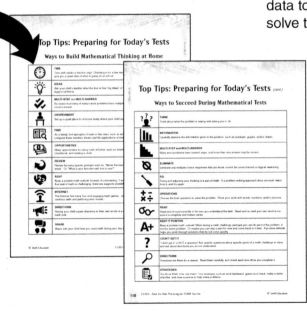

Practice Exercise 1

Directions: Read and solve each problem carefully. Record the correct answer on your answer sheet.

1. Which number shows $\frac{48}{100}$ in standard form?

   A 4,800

   B 4.8

   C 48,100

   (D) 0.48

---

2. A manager of a school cafeteria plans to serve hot dogs during lunch. If each package contains 8 hot dog buns, how many packages does he need to purchase to serve 146 hot dogs?

   (F) 17

   G 18

   H 19

   J 20

---

3. Which number could be filled in to make the comparison below true:

43,089,215 < _____

   A 42,589,231

   (B) 43,100,000

   C 43,088,216

   D 42,999,999

GO ON

Practice Exercise 1 *(cont.)*

Directions: Read and solve each problem carefully. Record the correct answer on your answer sheet.

4 Myra went to see a movie. The movie started at the time shown on the clock below. If the movie was 1 hour and 50 minutes long, what time did the movie end?

F 3:30 P.M.

G 3:40 P.M.

H 4:30 P.M.

J 4:40 P.M.

5 Choose the comparison that is true.

A $\frac{3}{4} > \frac{7}{8}$

B $\frac{1}{2} < \frac{5}{8}$

C $\frac{2}{3} < \frac{3}{8}$

D $\frac{7}{8} > \frac{9}{10}$

GO ON

Practice Exercise 1 (cont.)

Directions: Read and solve each problem carefully. Record the correct answer on your answer sheet.

6 Find the quotient for the division problem below.

$$486 \div 3$$

F 1,022

G 162

H 132

J 123

---

7 Use the model to help find the solution to the expression $0.03 + 0.9$.

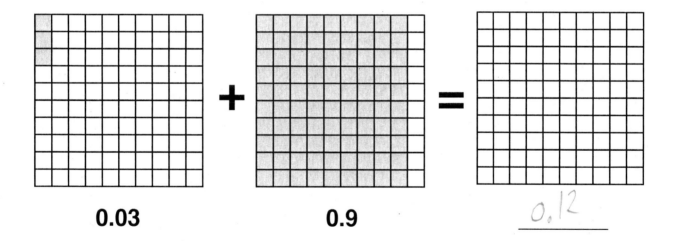

0.03   **0.9**   0.12

A 0.93

B 0.12

C 1.20

D 1.02

GO ON

Practice Exercise 1 *(cont.)*

Directions: Read and solve each problem carefully. Record the correct answer on your answer sheet.

---

8 Which of the shapes named does **NOT** have two sets of parallel lines?

    F Square

    G Rectangle

    H Trapezoid

    J Parallelogram

---

9 The value of the 7 in which number is 10 times the value of the seven in 34,579?

    A 63,257

    B 75,290

    C 124,872

    D 189,756

---

10 Find the product of 28 × 8. Fill in the correct bubbles on the answer sheet to record your answer.

66   160

226

STOP

Name: _____ Date: _____

Practice Exercise 2

Directions: Read and solve each problem carefully. Record the correct answer on your answer sheet.

1   Which number is 22,387 rounded to the nearest hundred?

   A 22,000

   B 22,300

   C 22,400

   D 22,380

2   Which expression shows 28,964,032 written in expanded form?

   F 20,000,000 + 8,000,000 + 900,000 + 60,000 + 4,000 + 32

   G 28,000,000 + 964,000 + 32

   H 28,000,000 + 900,000 + 60,000 + 4,000 + 30 + 2

   J 20,000,000 + 8,000,000 + 900,000 + 60,000 + 4,000 + 30 + 2

3   Choose the stem and leaf plot that correctly represents the data set below:

   | 14, 10, 16, 13, 14, 25, 27, 29, 42, 45, 46, 43, 31 |

   | 1|4 means 14. |

A

Stem	Leaf
1	0 3 4 4 6
2	5 7 9
3	1
4	2 3 5 6

B

Stem	Leaf
1	4 0 6 3
2	5 7 9
3	1
4	2 5 6

C

Stem	Leaf
1	0 1 6 3 4
2	2 5 7 9
3	0
4	2 5 6

D

Stem	Leaf
1	4 0 6 3
2	5 7 9 3
3	1 1
4	4 2 5 6

I don't get it

GO ON ➡

Practice Exercise 2 (cont.)

Directions: Read and solve each problem carefully. Record the correct answer on your answer sheet.

4   The area of a rectangular carpet is 96 square feet. The length of the carpet is 12 feet. What is the width of the carpet?

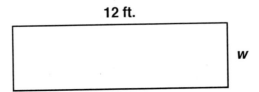

12 ft.

w

   F 8 feet

   G 12 feet

   H 24 feet

   J 36 feet

---

5   Which pair of fractions below are equivalent?

   A $\frac{1}{2}$ and $\frac{5}{8}$

   B $\frac{1}{2}$ and $\frac{7}{10}$

   C $\frac{3}{4}$ and $\frac{6}{8}$

   D $\frac{2}{3}$ and $\frac{5}{6}$

GO ON

Practice Exercise 2 *(cont.)*

Directions: Read and solve each problem carefully. Record the correct answer on your answer sheet.

6   What is the measure of the angle shown on the protractor below?

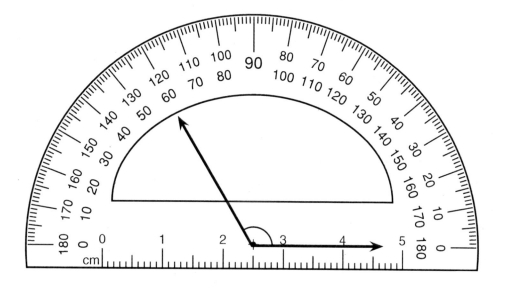

F 0º

G 60º

H 180º

J 120º

---

7   Sophia practices basketball by shooting 75 baskets twice a day. This means she will shoot *b* baskets in 7 days. Which equation below accurately models this situation?

A $b \times 2 \times 7 = 75$

B $75 \times 7 = b$

C $b = (75 \times 2) \times 7$

D $b \times 7 = 75 + 2$

GO ON

Practice Exercise 2 *(cont.)*

Directions: Read and solve each problem carefully. Record the correct answer on your answer sheet.

8 Which of the following is the correct product for 45 x 100?

   F 450

   G 4,500

   H 45,000

   J 4,545

---

9 Which number most accurately represents the point *P* on the number line?

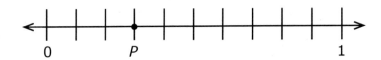

   A 0.3

   B 3

   C 0.03

   D 0.4

---

10 Paul bought 8 gallons of milk for his family. If a serving of milk is 1 cup, how many servings of milk did Paul buy? Fill in the correct bubbles on the answer sheet to record your answer.

Name: _____ Date: _____

Practice Exercise 3

Directions: Read and solve each problem carefully. Record the correct answer on your answer sheet.

1 Marcus ate $\frac{3}{8}$ of a cake and Kara ate $\frac{2}{8}$ of the same cake as shown on the model below. Which fraction accurately shows the total amount of cake remaining?

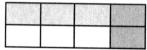

A $\frac{5}{8}$

B $\frac{3}{8}$

C $\frac{3}{16}$

D $\frac{3}{4}$

---

2 Choose the rule that accurately describes the pattern in the input-output table below.

Input	Output
35	43
43	51
51	59
59	67

F Subtract 7

G Add 9

H Add 7

J Add 8

---

3 How many lines of symmetry does the figure below have?

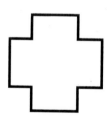

A 2

B 8

C 4

D 0

GO ON ➡

Practice Exercise 3 (cont.)

Directions: Read and solve each problem carefully. Record the correct answer on your answer sheet.

4 Theresa is baking muffins for the school bake sale. She bakes 94 muffins. Her friend Diego bakes 37 muffins. They plan to place 8 muffins in each box to sell. What is the greatest number of boxes that Theresa and Diego can completely fill?

F 131

H 132

G 16

J 17

---

5 A rectangle has an area of 24 square feet and a perimeter of 28 feet. Which pair of numbers could represent the width and length of the rectangle?

A 12 feet and 2 feet

C 4 feet and 7 feet

B 6 feet and 4 feet

D 3 feet and 8 feet

---

6 One way to decompose the fraction $\frac{5}{12}$ into smaller parts is modeled below. What is another way $\frac{5}{12}$ can be decomposed into smaller parts?

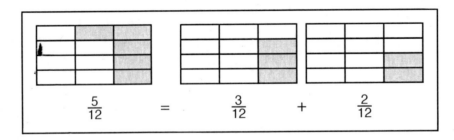

$$\frac{5}{12} \qquad = \qquad \frac{3}{12} \qquad + \qquad \frac{2}{12}$$

F $\frac{1}{12} + \frac{1}{12} + \frac{4}{12}$

G $\frac{1}{12} + \frac{1}{12} + \frac{3}{12}$

H $\frac{4}{12} + \frac{4}{12}$

J $\frac{1}{12} + \frac{1}{12} + \frac{1}{12} + \frac{1}{12}$

GO ON

Practice Exercise 3 (cont.)

Directions: Read and solve each problem carefully. Record the correct answer on your answer sheet.

7   Which data set is represented on the dot plot below

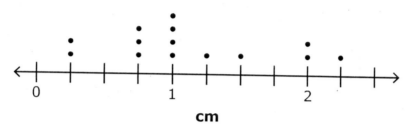

Lengths of Bees

cm

A $\frac{1}{4}, \frac{1}{4}, \frac{3}{4}, \frac{3}{4}, \frac{3}{4}, 1, 1, 1, 1\frac{1}{2}, 2, 2\frac{1}{4}$

B $\frac{1}{4}, \frac{3}{4}, 1, 1\frac{1}{4}, 1\frac{1}{2}, 2, 2\frac{1}{4}$

C $\frac{1}{4}, \frac{1}{2}, \frac{3}{4}, 1, 1\frac{1}{4}, 1\frac{1}{2}, 1\frac{3}{4}, 2, 2\frac{1}{4}$

D $\frac{1}{4}, \frac{1}{4}, \frac{3}{4}, \frac{3}{4}, \frac{3}{4}, 1, 1, 1, 1, 1\frac{1}{4}, 1\frac{1}{2}, 2, 2, 2\frac{1}{4}$

---

8   Which number is equivalent to four-tenths?

F   0.04

G $4\frac{1}{10}$

H   0.4

J   4.10

GO ON

Practice Exercise 3 *(cont.)*

Directions: Read and solve each problem carefully. Record the correct answer on your answer sheet.

9   The model below can be used to compare two decimals. Which comparison is true?

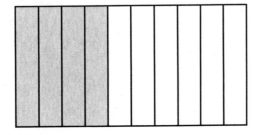 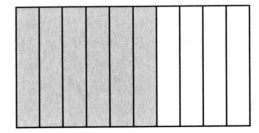

A 0.3 < 0.2

B 0.8 < 0.6

C 0.4 < 0.6

D 0.9 < 0.2

10   What is the difference between 543.19 and 235.89? Fill in the correct bubbles on the answer sheet to record your answer.

STOP

Name: _____   Date: _____

Practice Exercise 4

Directions: Read and solve each problem carefully. Record the correct answer on your answer sheet.

1   Which is the correct solution to 4,200 ÷ 6?

    A 7 tens

    B 700 hundreds

    C 7 hundreds

    D 700 tens

---

2   Students from two classes are attending a field trip to a museum. Each class is taking 20 students and 4 adults on the trip. They are traveling in vans that hold 9 people. Which equation below could be used to determine *v*, the number of vans necessary for the trip?

    F $(20 + 4) \div 9 = v$

    G $v = (20 + 4) \times 2 \div 9$

    H $(20 \times 2) + (4 \times 9) \div 2 = v$

    J $v = 4 \times 9 \times 2 \times 20$

---

3   There are 2 pans of brownies on the table as shown by the models below. $\frac{3}{10}$ of the brownies in one pan have been eaten, and $\frac{3}{5}$ of the brownies in the other pan have been eaten. Which comparison accurately describes the amount of brownies remaining?

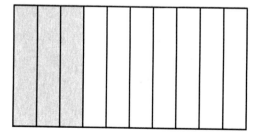   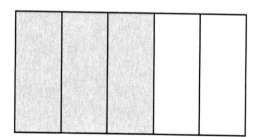

    A $\frac{3}{10} > \frac{3}{5}$

    B $\frac{3}{10} < \frac{3}{5}$

    C $\frac{7}{10} > \frac{2}{5}$

    D $\frac{7}{10} < \frac{3}{5}$

Practice Exercise 4 *(cont.)*

Directions: Read and solve each problem carefully. Record the correct answer on your answer sheet.

4   Which statement about the number 854,326.79 is true?

    F   The digit 4 has a value of (4×100)

    G   The digit 7 has a value of (7×0.01)

    H   The digit 2 has a value of $(2 \times 1,000)$

    J   The digit 3 has a value of (3×100)

---

5   Which of the following is an example of parallel lines?

    A

    B

    C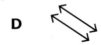

    D

GO ON

Practice Exercise 4 (cont.)

Directions: Read and solve each problem carefully. Record the correct answer on your answer sheet.

6   The table below shows the number of players being placed on basketball teams. If the pattern continues, how many teams will be needed for 96 players?

Total Players	Number of Teams
16	2
40	5
64	8
96	

F 10

G 12

H 11

J 14

7   Which statement about all parallelograms is true?

A All parallelograms have four right angles.

B All parallelograms have two obtuse and two acute angles.

C All parallelograms have two sets of parallel lines.

D All parallelograms have exactly one pair of parallel lines.

Practice Exercise 4 *(cont.)*

Directions: Read and solve each problem carefully. Record the correct answer on your answer sheet.

8   What is the measure of the angle on the protractor shown below?

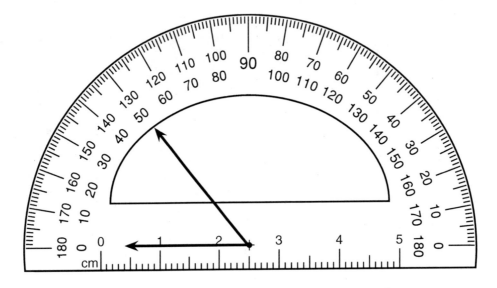

    F   180º   **H**   130º

    G   50º   **J**   60º

---

9   Which of the following must be true about the solution to $\frac{1}{2} + \frac{3}{4}$?

    A   The solution is greater than 1.

    B   The solution is greater than 2.

    C   The solution is less than 1.

    D   The solution is exactly 1.

---

10   A small truck weighs 3 tons. A large car weighs 5,893 pounds. What is the difference in pounds between the truck and the car? Fill in the correct bubbles on the answer sheet to record your answer.

Practice Exercise 5

Directions: Read and solve each problem carefully. Record the correct answer on your answer sheet.

1   Which of the following shows 0.42 written as a fraction?

   A $4\frac{2}{100}$

   B $4\frac{2}{10}$

   C $\frac{42}{100}$

   D $\frac{42}{1000}$

---

2   Which addition problem is modeled by the number line?

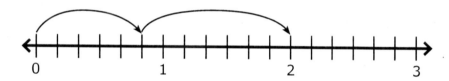

   F $1 + 1 = 2$

   G $\frac{5}{6} + \frac{7}{6} = 2$

   H $5 + 7 = 12$

   J $\frac{3}{4} + \frac{5}{4} = 2$

---

3   What would be a good estimate for the measure of the angle below?

   A 270º

   B 8º

   C 40º

   D 120º

GO ON

Practice Exercise 5 *(cont.)*

Directions: Read and solve each problem carefully. Record the correct answer on your answer sheet.

4   A square sandbox has a length of 7 meters. What is the perimeter of the sandbox?

    F 14 meters   **H** 49 meters

    G 28 meters   **J** 7 meters

---

5   Mike ran 1.52 miles on Monday and 2.7 miles on Tuesday. What is the total distance Mike ran over the two days?

    A 4.59 miles   **C** 1.79 miles

    B 3.59 miles   **D** 4.22 miles

---

6   Choose the number line that could be used to accurately round 4,374 to the nearest 100.

F
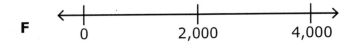

G
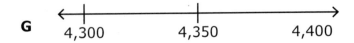

H
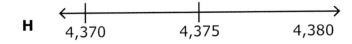

J
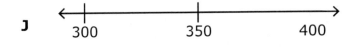

GO ON

Name: _____ Date: _____

Practice Exercise 5 (cont.)

Directions: Read and solve each problem carefully. Record the correct answer on your answer sheet.

7 Andrea has 132 stickers. She decides to give her stickers to 7 friends. Andrea wants to give each friend the same number of stickers. How many stickers will Andrea have left?

A 4

B 5

C 6

D 7

---

8 Which data set matches the frequency table below?

Frequency Class	Frequency
0–20	4
21–40	7
41–60	0
61–80	1
81–100	7

F 2, 4, 0, 1, 5

G 17, 19, 27, 28, 29, 32, 75, 82, 85, 87, 92, 96

H 13, 16, 19, 19, 23, 24, 25, 25, 26, 27, 27, 63, 82, 83, 84, 85, 86, 86, 94

J 19, 20, 25, 26, 27, 28, 28, 29, 42, 62, 62, 81

GO ON

Practice Exercise 5 (cont.)

Directions: Read and solve each problem carefully. Record the correct answer on your answer sheet.

9   Theresa bought an old bike. She repaired the bike and painted it a new color. Theresa then sold the bike at a garage sale. She made this list to keep track of what she did.

> - $15.00: amount paid for old bike
> - $8.50: amount paid for bike repairs
> - $5.00: cost of paint
> - $45.00: selling price

What was Theresa's profit from selling the bike?

A $45.00

B $28.50

C $73.50

D $16.50

10   A manager at a theater is reserving seats for adults and children. There are 7 rows reserved for adults and 5 rows reserved for children. Each adult row has 14 seats. Each row for children has 16 seats. How many total seats are reserved in the theater? Fill in the correct bubbles on the answer sheet to record your answer.

STOP

Name: _____ Date: _____

Practice Exercise 6

Directions: Read and solve each problem carefully. Record the correct answer on your answer sheet.

1 Which decimal represents the shaded section below?

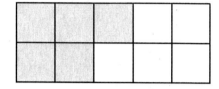

    A 5.0

    B 0.05

    C 0.5

    D 5.00

---

2 Which number shows an equivalent for 3.25?

    F $3\frac{25}{10}$

    G $3\frac{25}{100}$

    H 325

    J $\frac{32}{5}$

---

3 Which quadrilateral has exactly one pair of parallel lines?

    A Rhombus

    B Trapezoid

    C Parallelogram

    D Square

GO ON ➡

Practice Exercise 6 (cont.)

Directions: Read and solve each problem carefully. Record the correct answer on your answer sheet.

---

4   Which number is 40,000 + 3,000 + 50 + 9?

    F 43,509   **H** 45,309

    G 43,095   **J** 43,059

---

5   Angle *SRW* measures 130º. Use the given information to determine the measure of angle *SRT*.

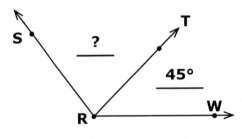

    A 85º   **C** 45º

    B 175º   **D** 125º

---

6   The table shows a relationship between the input numbers and the output numbers generated by a number machine.

Input	Output
5	250
6	300
7	350
8	400

Which number machine shows the same relationship as the one shown in the table?

F 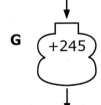   **G** 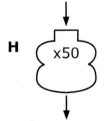   **H** 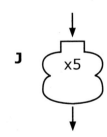   **J** x5

GO ON

Practice Exercise 6 *(cont.)*

Directions: Read and solve each problem carefully. Record the correct answer on your answer sheet.

It's Tea Time

Ingredients

1½ cups flour
2 teaspoons baking powder
½ teaspoon baking soda
1 cup sugar
1½ sticks cold butter, cut into ¼-inch pieces
½ cup heavy cream
½ teaspoon salt
honey

What You Do

Sift the dry ingredients and place them in a large mixer. Add the cold butter. Mix on low speed until the butter breaks into pea-sized pieces. Add the cream. Once the dough comes together, flatten it onto a sheet tray and freeze it. Cut the dough into squares. Place the squares on a tray lined with a baking mat. Bake at 325°F for 25 minutes. After the scones cool, drizzle them with honey.

Source: Jim Scherer   Image: Getty Images

7   How many cups of flour are needed to triple the recipe for scones?

A 3

B $3\frac{1}{2}$

C 4

D $4\frac{1}{2}$

8   How many teaspoons of baking powder are needed to triple the recipe for scones?

F $1\frac{1}{2}$

G 5

H 6

J $7\frac{1}{2}$

GO ON ➡

Practice Exercise 6 (cont.)

Directions: Read and solve each problem carefully. Record the correct answer on your answer sheet.

9   Which real-life object can hold only 5 liters of liquid?

A

B

C

D

10   An office manager plans to buy 3 computers. The price of each computer is $1,000. The manager agrees to pay a total of $2,483, and will pay the remaining amount at a later date. How much more money must the manager pay for the computers? Fill in the correct bubbles on the answer sheet to record your answer.

STOP

Name: _____ Date: _____

Practice Exercise 7

Directions: Read and solve each problem carefully. Record the correct answer on your answer sheet.

1   Jadon used part of a loaf of bread to make his lunch. His brother opened an identical loaf of bread and used some of it to make his lunch. The models are shaded to represent the bread each boy ate.

Jadon: ▢▢▢▢▢   Jadon's Brother: ▢▢▢▢▢

What fraction of the loaves of bread was eaten?

A $\frac{1}{5}$ **C** $\frac{4}{5}$

B $1\frac{1}{10}$ **D** $1\frac{1}{5}$

---

2   A farmer picked the apples in the baskets below to sell at a local market. The farmer plans to sell the apples in bags with 6 apples in each bag. How many full bags can the farmer make?

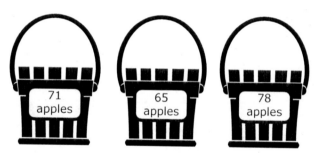

71 apples   65 apples   78 apples

F 35   **H** 39

G 36   **J** 41

---

3   Beth is borrowing money from the bank to buy a house. She will have to pay back the money that she borrowed. Which statement describes the payments?

A Fixed expenses, because the payments will be done after two months.

B Variable expenses, because the amount for each payment changes.

C Fixed expenses, because the payments are usually the same amount each month.

D Variable expenses, because the payments will not be due every month.

GO ON

Name: _____   Date: _____

Practice Exercise 7 (cont.)

Directions: Read and solve each problem carefully. Record the correct answer on your answer sheet.

4   Marilyn is reading a book. She read a total of 3 times as many pages on Tuesday and Wednesday as she read on Monday. If Marilyn read p pages on Monday, which diagram represents the number of pages she read on Tuesday and Wednesday?

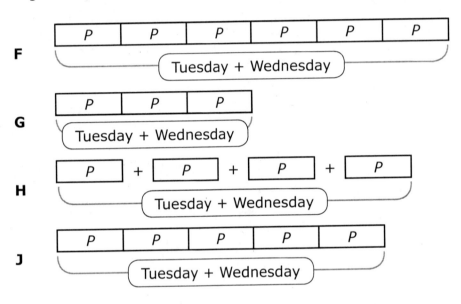

5   Which line segments in the figure below appear to parallel?

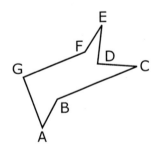

A Line segments *ED* and *DC*

B Line segments *GF* and *ED*

C Line segments *AB* and *AG*

D Line segments *GF* and *BC*

© Shell Education

Practice Exercise 7 (cont.)

Directions: Read and solve each problem carefully. Record the correct answer on your answer sheet.

6 Which data set is represented by the stem and leaf plot below?

Stem	Leaf
0	6 8 9
1	2 4 4 7 9
2	3 4
3	0
4	8 9
5	0

1|2 means 12.

F 80, 90, 24, 24, 27, 29, 23, 24, 30, 48, 49, 50

G 8, 9, 12, 44, 79, 23, 24, 30, 48, 9, 50

H 6, 8, 9, 12, 14, 14, 17, 19, 23, 24, 30, 48, 49, 50

J 0, 1, 2, 3, 4, 5, 8, 9, 2, 4, 4, 7, 9, 3, 4, 8, 9

7 The area of a rectangular bedroom is 288 square feet. The length of the bedroom is 16 feet. What is the width of the bedroom?

A 15 feet

B 18 feet

C 272 feet

D 4,608 feet

8 A puppy at a shelter weighs 7 pounds, 12 ounces. How many total ounces does the puppy weigh?

F 19 ounces

G 84 ounces

H 112 ounces

J 124 ounces

GO ON

Practice Exercise 7 *(cont.)*

Directions: Read and solve each problem carefully. Record the correct answer on your answer sheet.

9   Look at the area model below.

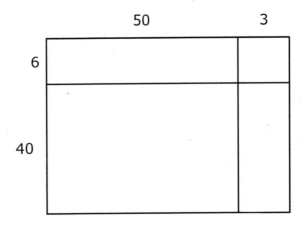

Which expression does the model represent?

A (40 × 50) + (6 × 50)

B (6 × 50) + (6 × 3) + (40 × 50) + (40 × 3)

C (50 × 6 × 3 × 40)

D (50 × 40) + (40 × 3)

---

10   Reed bought new clothes for baseball. He bought pants that costs $59.86 and two shirts that cost $18.56 each. What is the total amount of money Reed spent? Fill in the correct bubbles on the answer sheet to record your answer.

Practice Exercise 8

Directions: Read and solve each problem carefully. Record the correct answer on your answer sheet.

1 What is the measure of the angle shown to the nearest degree?

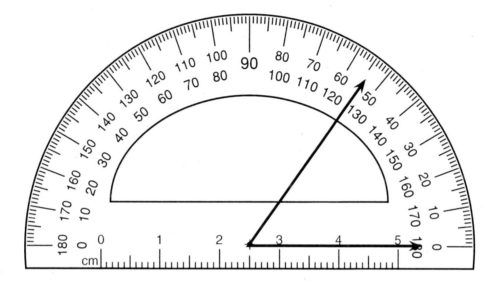

A 76°

B 54°

C 116°

D 58°

---

2 Connor and his mom went shopping for school clothes. He wanted 3 shirts that cost $18 each, and 2 pairs of pants that cost $12 each. If Connor's mom paid for the clothes with a $100 bill, how much money did she get back?

F $32

G $22

H $18

J $28

GO ON

Practice Exercise 8 (cont.)

Directions: Read and solve each problem carefully. Record the correct answer on your answer sheet.

3 Which statement is true about this figure?

A All angles are congruent.

B All angles are right angles.

C There are exactly two pairs of parallel lines.

D There are exactly two pairs of perpendicular lines.

---

4 Which angles in the following figure are right angles?

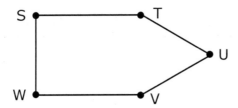

F Angles *T* and *V*

G Angles *S* and *U*

H Angles *S* and *W*

J Angles *W* and *U*

---

5 The fraction $\frac{5}{12}$ can be represented by this expression:

$$\frac{1}{12} + \frac{1}{12} + \frac{1}{12} + \frac{1}{12} + \bigcirc$$

What needs to go in the ⬠ to complete the expression?

A $\frac{4}{12}$

B $\frac{4}{48}$

C $\frac{1}{48}$

D $\frac{1}{12}$

GO ON ➡

Practice Exercise 8 *(cont.)*

Directions: Read and solve each problem carefully. Record the correct answer on your answer sheet.

6 Xavier and Ashton are reading the same book. Xavier has read $\frac{7}{10}$ and claims that this is more than the amount Ashton read, which is $\frac{3}{4}$. Ashton disagrees and says that $\frac{3}{4}$ is more. Which student is correct?

F Xavier, because  has more parts colored than

G Xavier, because 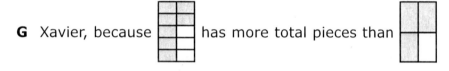 has more total pieces than

H Ashton, because

J Neither, because

---

7 Which number below is equivalent to 3.45?

A 345

B 345,000

C $3\frac{4}{5}$

D $3\frac{45}{100}$

GO ON

Practice Exercise 8 *(cont.)*

Directions: Read and solve each problem carefully. Record the correct answer on your answer sheet.

8 Select the number that does **NOT** round to 23,500 when rounded to the nearest hundred.

    F 23,451

    G 23,500

    H 23,551

    J 23,549

---

9 What is the value of the 7 in the number below?

84,567.23

    A 700

    B 70

    C 7

    D $\frac{1}{7}$

---

10 The dimensions of a garden are 12 feet by 28 feet. What is the area, in square feet, of the garden? Fill in the correct bubbles on the answer sheet to record your answer.

STOP

 51703—Time For Kids: Practicing for STAAR Success

Practice Exercise 9

Directions: Read and solve each problem carefully. Record the correct answer on your answer sheet.

1 Find the sum of 89.73 and 246.51.

    A 156.77   **C** 336.24

    B 225.56   **D** 1,143.85

---

2 What number best represents point *A* on the number line?

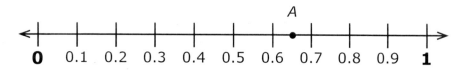

    F 6.7   **H** 65

    G $\frac{1}{6}$ **J** 0.65

---

3 The models below can be used to represent an addition problem. What is the sum of the problem represented by the models?

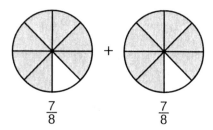

$$\frac{7}{8} \quad + \quad \frac{7}{8}$$

    A $\frac{14}{16}$

    B $\frac{14}{8}$

    C $2\frac{7}{8}$

    D $\frac{16}{14}$

GO ON

Practice Exercise 9 (cont.)

Directions: Read and solve each problem carefully. Record the correct answer on your answer sheet.

4   Which expression below shows 39.08 written in expanded form?

   F 30 + 9 + 0.0 + 0.08

   G 3,000 + 900 + 0 + 8

   H 39 + 0.08

   J 30 + 9 + 0 + 0.8

---

5   An African elephant ate 432 pounds of food on Monday. On Tuesday and Wednesday, the elephant ate 323 pounds of food each day. Which equation could be used to find how many total pounds of food, *f*, were eaten over the three days?

   A 323 + 423 = *f*

   B (2 × 323) + 432 = *f*

   C (432 × 2) + 323 = *f*

   D 323 + 323 + 323 = *f*

---

6   Jeremiah keeps his money in a financial institution so that it will stay safe. When he brings money to the institution to add to his account, he will be making a —

   F Transfer

   G Deposit

   H Withdrawal

   J Interest

GO ON

Name: _____ Date: _____

Practice Exercise 9 *(cont.)*

Directions: Read and solve each problem carefully. Record the correct answer on your answer sheet.

7   Using the line plot below, determine the total time spent completing homework by students who spent $\frac{3}{4}$ of an hour on homework.

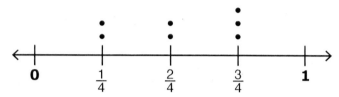

Time to Complete Last Night's Homework

A $\frac{3}{4}$ hour

B $1\frac{1}{4}$ hours

C $2\frac{1}{4}$ hours

D $2\frac{3}{4}$ hours

8   Which of the shapes below does **NOT** have any right angles?

F

G

H

J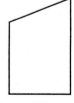

GO ON ▶

Practice Exercise 9 *(cont.)*

Directions: Read and solve each problem carefully. Record the correct answer on your answer sheet.

9 An input-output table is shown below. Which expression could be used to determine the 20th output of the table?

Input	Output
3	1
6	2
9	3
12	4
15	5

A $20 \div 3$

B $(20 \times 5) \div 3$

C $(20 \div 3) \times 5$

D $(20 \times 3) \div 3$

10 A total of 350 water bottles is expected to be sold at a soccer tournament. The tournament manager plans to order 15 cases of water. Each case of water contains 24 bottles. How many extra water bottles will the manager have? Fill in the correct bubbles on the answer sheet to record your answer.

STOP

Practice Exercise 10

Directions: Read and solve each problem carefully. Record the correct answer on your answer sheet.

1 What number could be used to describe the shaded section in the model?

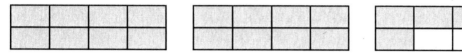

A $\frac{21}{24}$

B $2\frac{5}{8}$

C 2.58

D $\frac{3}{24}$

---

2 The model below represents a vegetable garden in Timothy's backyard. Timothy wants to keep the deer out of his garden, so he is going to put up fencing. Use the model to determine the amount of fencing Timothy will need.

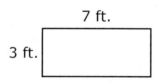

7 ft.

3 ft.

F 10 feet

G 21 square feet

H 20 feet

J 21 feet

---

3 Evan and Antonio each ordered a medium cheese pizza from the same restaurant. Evan ate more of his pizza. Which comparison below could correctly model the amount of pizza eaten by Evan compared to the amount eaten by Antonio?

A $\frac{1}{2} > \frac{3}{4}$

B $\frac{3}{8} > \frac{1}{2}$

C $\frac{3}{4} < \frac{7}{8}$

D $\frac{2}{3} > \frac{3}{4}$

GO ON

Name: _____ Date: _____

Practice Exercise 10 (cont.)

Directions: Read and solve each problem carefully. Record the correct answer on your answer sheet.

4   Lucy had a lemonade stand. The details of Lucy's lemonade stand are listed.

> • Lemonade mix: $4.99
>
> • Cups: $2.99
>
> • Price of lemonade: 75 cents a cup

Lucy sold 15 cups of lemonade. What was her profit?

F $19.23

G $11.25

H $7.98

J $3.27

---

5   To get to school, Zachary took a route that was 2 miles long. Zachary walked to school every day and walked home from school 3 days a week. Assuming Zachary had 2 full weeks (5 days each week) of school, how many miles did he walk?

A 16 miles

B 32 miles

C 20 miles

D 50 miles

Practice Exercise 10 *(cont.)*

Directions: Read and solve each problem carefully. Record the correct answer on your answer sheet.

6 Which shape has exactly 2 lines of symmetry?

F

H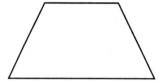

G

J

---

7 The frequency table below displays the length of a group of fourth graders' thumbs, measured to the nearest $\frac{1}{2}$ cm. Which data set could be the one represented in the table?

Length of Thumb	Frequency
0–1	0
$1\frac{1}{2}$–$2\frac{1}{2}$	1
3–4	2
$4\frac{1}{2}$–$5\frac{1}{2}$	7
8	5

A 1, 2, 7, 5

B 0, 1, $1\frac{1}{2}$, $2\frac{1}{2}$, 3, 4, $4\frac{1}{2}$, 5, $5\frac{1}{2}$

C 2, $3\frac{1}{2}$, 4, $4\frac{1}{2}$, $4\frac{1}{2}$, $4\frac{1}{2}$, 5, 5, 5, $5\frac{1}{2}$, 8, 8, 8, 8, 8

D $\frac{1}{2}$, $1\frac{1}{2}$, $2\frac{1}{2}$, $2\frac{1}{2}$, 3, 3, 4, $4\frac{1}{2}$, $4\frac{1}{2}$, $5\frac{1}{2}$

GO ON

Practice Exercise 10 *(cont.)*

Directions: Read and solve each problem carefully. Record the correct answer on your answer sheet.

8   Which protractor has an angle closest to 90 degrees?

F

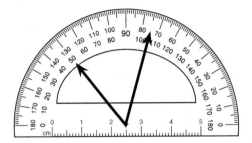

H

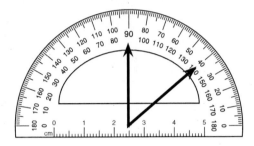

G

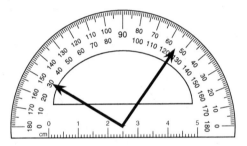

J

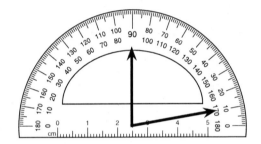

---

9   What is the solution to the expression?

| 100 × 58 |

A 58,000

B 580

C 5,008

D 5,800

---

10   What is the sum of 45.06 and 225.9? Fill in the correct bubbles on the answer sheet to record your answer.

STOP

Practice Exercise 11

Directions: Read and solve each problem carefully. Record the correct answer on your answer sheet.

1   The model represents the subtraction problem: $1 - \frac{5}{12}$

X	X	
X		
X		
X		

What is the solution to this subtraction problem?

A $\frac{7}{12}$

B $\frac{5}{12}$

C 1

D $1\frac{5}{12}$

---

2   A group is going on a boating trip. Each boat can hold 4 passengers. If there are 155 people on the trip, how many boats will be needed so that everyone can participate?

F 37

G 39

H 620

J 40

---

3   A local university has 23,945 students. What is the enrollment of the university rounded to the nearest thousand?

A 20,000

B 23,900

C 24,000

D 30,000

GO ON

Practice Exercise 11 (cont.)

Directions: Read and solve each problem carefully. Record the correct answer on your answer sheet.

4 In the number 621,245,783.9, what is the value of the 5?

F 5

G 50,000

H 5,783.9

J 5,000

---

5 Gabriel planned to spend exactly three months hiking the Appalachian Trail. The trail is 2,189 miles long. In the first month, Gabriel hiked 647 miles. He wants to split the distance he has remaining equally between the 2 months. Which equation will help him determine, d, the distance he has to walk each month?

A $2,189 - d = 647$

B $2,189 - 647 = d$

C $(2,189 - 647) \div 2 = d$

D $d = 2,189 - (647 \times 2)$

---

6 Which shape does **NOT** have obtuse angles?

F

H

G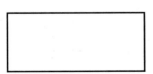

J

GO ON

Name: _____ Date: _____

Practice Exercise 11 *(cont.)*

Directions: Read and solve each problem carefully. Record the correct answer on your answer sheet.

7 Which of the comparisons below is **NOT** true?

A $\frac{3}{4} > \frac{1}{2}$

B $\frac{9}{10} > \frac{5}{6}$

C $\frac{2}{3} > \frac{7}{8}$

D $\frac{11}{10} > \frac{9}{10}$

---

8 Ms. Mundy has a number box. She inputs a number into the box. The box then applies a rule before providing an output. A selection of these inputs and outputs is shown below. Which could be the rule applied to the inputs by the Number Box?

Ms. Mundy's Number Box

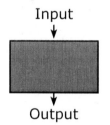

Input

Output

Input	Output
1	25
2	50
3	75
4	100
5	125

F Add 24

G Multiply by 25

H Add 25

J Multiply by 4

GO ON ➡

Practice Exercise 11 *(cont.)*

Directions: Read and solve each problem carefully. Record the correct answer on your answer sheet.

9 Which representation below shows 40 cents?

A

B

C

D

---

10 What is the quotient of 847 divided by 7? Fill in the correct bubbles on the answer sheet to record your answer.

Name: _____ Date: _____

Practice Exercise 12

Directions: Read and solve each problem carefully. Record the correct answer on your answer sheet.

1 What is the best estimate for the measure of the angle shown below?

A 110º

B 80º

C 90º

D 140º

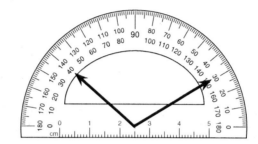

---

2 Lydia made trail mix using peanuts, raisins, and chocolate candies.

> $\frac{2}{10}$ of the trail mix was peanuts
>
> $\frac{6}{10}$ of the trail mix was raisins
>
> The rest of the trail mix was chocolate candies

What fraction of the trail mix was chocolate candies?

F $\frac{4}{10}$, because $\frac{6}{10} - \frac{2}{10} = \frac{4}{10}$ **H** $\frac{2}{10}$, because $\frac{2}{10} + \frac{6}{10} = \frac{8}{10}$ and $1 - \frac{8}{10} = \frac{2}{10}$

G $\frac{8}{10}$, because $\frac{2}{10} + \frac{6}{10} = \frac{8}{10}$ **J** $\frac{12}{10}$, because $\frac{6}{10} + \frac{2}{10} + \frac{6}{10} = \frac{12}{10}$

---

3 A stem and leaf plot is shown. Which data set matches the data in the stem and leaf plot?

Stem	Leaf
0	3 4 5
1	2 5 6 6
2	
3	4 7 9 9
4	0 1
5	2 3 4

3|4 means 34.

A 30, 40, 50, 21, 25, 26, 26, 43, 47, 49, 49, 04, 14, 52, 53, 54

B 3, 12, 40, 52, 53, 41, 37, 15, 4, 5, 16, 39, 54, 39, 16, 34

C 3, 4, 5, 2, 5, 6, 6, 4, 7, 9, 9, 0, 1, 2, 3, 4

D 0, 1, 2, 3, 4, 5, 3, 4, 5, 2, 5, 6, 6, 4, 7, 9, 9, 0, 1, 2, 3, 4

GO ON

Practice Exercise 12 (cont.)

Directions: Read and solve each problem carefully. Record the correct answer on your answer sheet.

4   Which set of numbers below is correctly ordered from least to greatest?

   F 32,456, 31,999, 31,998   **H** 12,009, 11,999, 11,900

   G 32,556, 33,000, 32,456   **J** 32,456, 32,556, 33,000

---

5   Alison has a goal of running 5,000 miles over 4 years. Her data for the first three years is in the list below:

> - 945 miles the first year
> - 1,634 miles the second year
> - 1,430 miles the third year

How many miles does Alison need to run during the fourth year in order to reach her goal?

   A 4,069   **C** 1,250

   B 991   **D** 1,931

---

6   The table below shows a pattern in which the position can be used to determine the input, which can then be used to determine the output.

Position	Input	Output
1	3	15
2	4	20
3	5	25
4	6	30

Assuming this pattern continues, what will be the output for the number in position 15?

   F 80

   G 85

   H 27

   J 105

GO ON

Name: _____ Date: _____

Practice Exercise 12 *(cont.)*

Directions: Read and solve each problem carefully. Record the correct answer on your answer sheet.

Popular Dog Names

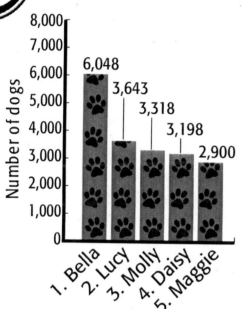

Female Dog Names

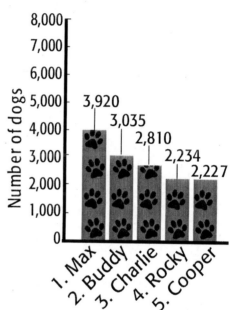

Male Dog Names

Sources: *TIME For Kids* and Veterinary Pet Insurance CO.

7 How many fewer people named their dogs Rocky compared with those who named their dogs Lucy?

    A 833   **C** 1,419

    B 1,409   **D** 5,877

8 How many people chose dog names that begin with the letter M?

    F 6,218   **H** 9,138

    G 7,238   **J** 10,138

GO ON ▶

Practice Exercise 12 (cont.)

Directions: Read and solve each problem carefully. Record the correct answer on your answer sheet.

9   The fraction $\frac{7}{8}$, and one way to decompose it into smaller parts, are shown.

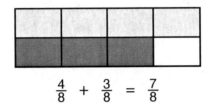

$$\frac{4}{8} \;+\; \frac{3}{8} \;=\; \frac{7}{8}$$

Which choice is **NOT** an accurate way to decompose $\frac{7}{8}$?

A $\frac{1}{8} + \frac{1}{8} + \frac{1}{8} + \frac{1}{8} + \frac{1}{8} + \frac{2}{8}$

B $\frac{1}{8} + \frac{2}{8} + \frac{3}{8}$

C $\frac{2}{8} + \frac{2}{8} + \frac{3}{8}$

D $\frac{6}{8} + \frac{1}{8}$

---

10   As part of his training for an upcoming race, James ran 5,500 meters. What distance did James run in kilometers? Fill in the correct bubbles on the answer sheet to record your answer.

STOP

Practice Exercise 13

Directions: Read and solve each problem carefully. Record the correct answer on your answer sheet.

1   Which shape does **NOT** have obtuse angles?

 **A**

C

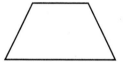 **B**

D

---

2   A rectangle is pictured. If one side of the rectangle measures 14 feet and the perimeter is 50 feet, what is the measurement of the other dimension?

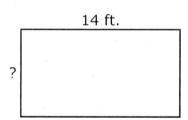

14 ft.

?

F 22 feet   **H** 11 feet

G 36 feet   **J** 18 feet

---

3   A number line is pictured below.

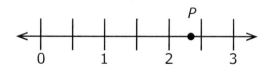

P

0   1   2   3

Which number best represents point *P* on the number line?

A 2.4   **C** 0.24

B 0.2   **D** 0.4

GO ON

Practice Exercise 13 (cont.)

Directions: Read and solve each problem carefully. Record the correct answer on your answer sheet.

4 Which number fits the statement below?

The digit 5 has a value of (5 × 1,000)

F 2,534.3

G 385,023

H 498.05

J 4,065.02

---

5 Which comparison below is **NOT** true?

A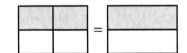

C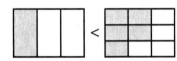

B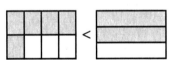

D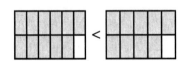

---

6 A bag can hold 18 apples. A farmer recently picked 45 bags of apples. How many apples did the farmer pick?

F 45

G 18

H 63

J 810

GO ON

Practice Exercise 13 *(cont.)*

Directions: Read and solve each problem carefully. Record the correct answer on your answer sheet.

7 Alanna collects stamps. In her collection, she had 1,765 stamps. She decided to put 872 stamps in storage for safe keeping. She put the remaining stamps into protective sheets that could hold 9 stamps each. How many protective sheets did Alanna use?

    A 100

    B 101

    C 893

    D 197

---

8 What is the area for the figure shown?

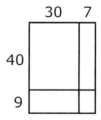

    F 733

    G 1,367

    H 1,813

    J 1,263

GO ON

Name: _____ Date: _____

Practice Exercise 13 *(cont.)*

Directions: Read and solve each problem carefully. Record the correct answer on your answer sheet.

9

Position	Input	Output
1	5	2
2	10	7
3	15	12
4	20	17

Given the input-output table above, which choice correctly describes what is done to the position, then the input, to get the output?

A Multiply the position by 2

B Multiply the position by 5, then subtract 3

C Multiply the position by 5

D Multiply the position by 4, then subtract 2

---

10 If the numbers in the addition problem 251 + 548 are rounded to the nearest 10, what is the estimated sum? Fill in the correct bubbles on the answer sheet to record your answer.

Practice Exercise 14

Directions: Read and solve each problem carefully. Record the correct answer on your answer sheet.

1 To gather the data for the dot plot below, how many people were surveyed?

Shoe Sizes

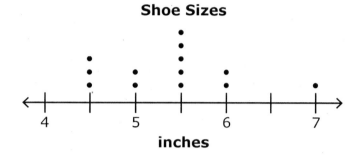

inches

A 7   **C** 5

B 13   **D** 6

---

2 Sarah ran 645 yards on Monday. On Tuesday, she added 135 yards to the route she took Monday. What distance in yards did Sarah run over the two days?

F 780 yards   **H** 880 yards

G 510 yards   **J** 1,425 yards

---

3 At a pizza party, there were 3 pizzas of the same size each cut into 16 slices. The model below represents the 3 full pizzas.

  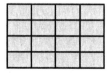

If $2\frac{3}{16}$ pizzas were eaten, how much pizza was left over?

A $\frac{13}{16}$ **C** 1

B $\frac{3}{4}$ **D** $\frac{48}{16}$

GO ON

Practice Exercise 14 *(cont.)*

Directions: Read and solve each problem carefully. Record the correct answer on your answer sheet.

4   What is another way to write 2.25?

    F 225

    G $2\frac{3}{4}$

    H $2\frac{25}{4}$

    J $2\frac{25}{100}$

---

5   Which triangle below does **NOT** have a right angle?

    A   **C**

    B 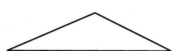   **D**

---

6   What is the closest measurement for the length of this paper clip?

    F 5 centimeters

    G 7 centimeters

    H 2 centimeters

    J 50 centimeters

GO ON ➡

Name: _____ Date: _____

Practice Exercise 14 *(cont.)*

Directions: Read and solve each problem carefully. Record the correct answer on your answer sheet.

Wool Producers

1. **Australia** 408,517
2. **China** 401,243
3. **New Zealand** 197,580
4. **United Kingdom** 72,083
5. **Argentina** 67,782

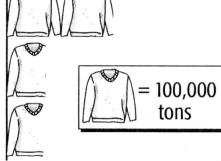
= 100,000 tons

7 Which is the best estimate for the difference, in tons, between the amount of wool produced in New Zealand and the amount of wool produced in Argentina?

A 130,000

B 190,000

C 210,000

D 270,000

8 How many tons of wool are made by the top two wool producers?

F 408,517

G 401,423

H 809,940

J 67,782

GO ON

Practice Exercise 14 *(cont.)*

Directions: Read and solve each problem carefully. Record the correct answer on your answer sheet.

9 Which comparison below is true?

A $\frac{2}{3} < \frac{3}{4}$

B $\frac{9}{10} < \frac{5}{6}$

C $\frac{5}{6} > \frac{9}{10}$

D $\frac{3}{4} < \frac{1}{2}$

---

10 In the number below, what is the value of the digit 2? Fill in the correct bubbles on the answer sheet to record your answer.

$$4{,}398{,}327.09$$

Practice Exercise 15

Directions: Read and solve each problem carefully. Record the correct answer on your answer sheet.

1   What is the difference between the perimeters of the two rectangles pictured?

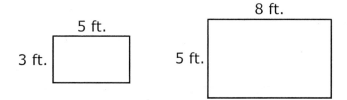

    A 25 feet   **C** 5 feet

    B 2 feet   **D** 10 feet

---

2   Which answer shows the number below written in standard form?

80,000,000 + 9,000,000 + 40,000 + 2,000 + 100 + 20

    F 89,421,200

    G 89,042,120

    H 89,042,102

    J 809,042,120

---

3   Each month, Frank needs to pay the water bill, the electricity bill, the mortgage, and the heat bill. Which one of these expenses is most likely a fixed expense?

    A The water bill

    B The electricity bill

    C The mortgage

    D The heat bill

GO ON

Practice Exercise 15 *(cont.)*

Directions: Read and solve each problem carefully. Record the correct answer on your answer sheet.

4 Kaitlyn and Aiden both play soccer. The details about their practices are below:

> • Kaitlyn practices 4 days a week for an hour and a half
> • Aiden practices 3 days a week for an hour and 45 minutes

How much more time each week does Kaitlyn spend practicing than Aiden?

F 15 minutes   **H** 45 minutes

G 20 minutes   **J** 1 hour

---

5 Michael loves to chew gum. The input-output table shows the relationship between the number of pieces of gum Michael has, *p*, and the number of pieces he has chewed, *c*. The output is $p - 6$.

Input	p	12	13	14	15
Output	c	6	7	8	9

How many pieces will Michael have chewed when he has 28 pieces?

A 34   **C** 22

B 6   **D** 15

---

6 Jeremiah has $543.23 in a savings account. He wants to spend $222.98 on a new gaming machine. If he does this, how much money will Jeremiah have left?

F $766.21

G $221.75

H $320.00

J $320.25

Practice Exercise 15 (cont.)

Directions: Read and solve each problem carefully. Record the correct answer on your answer sheet.

7 What is the quotient of 3,255 divided by 5?

   A 651

   B 16,275

   C 3,250

   D 6,051

---

8 Which protractor has an angle that appears to be 115 degrees?

F

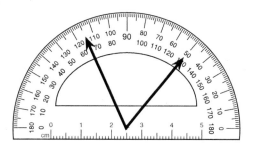

H

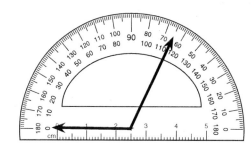

G

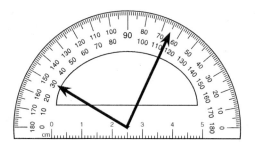

J

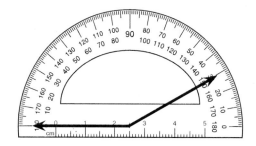

GO ON

Practice Exercise 15 *(cont.)*

Directions: Read and solve each problem carefully. Record the correct answer on your answer sheet.

9   A chef in a restaurant needs 12 quarts of water to prepare the soup of the day. How many pints of water are needed?

   A 48

   B 24

   C 6

   D 36

---

10   Use the diagram below to determine the measure of angle *ADE.* Fill in the correct bubbles on the answer sheet to record your answer.

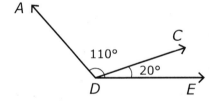

STOP

Practice Exercise 16

Directions: Read and solve each problem carefully. Record the correct answer on your answer sheet.

1 Which shape below has exactly three sets of parallel lines?

A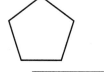

C

B

D

---

2 Kyle has a part-time job at a restaurant where he works 16 hours a week. If Kyle works for 52 weeks, how many hours will he have worked in all?

F 68

G 832

H 36

J 960

---

3 The data set below shows the number of different houses the students in a fourth-grade class have lived in. Which frequency table represents this data?

4,1,1,1,1,1,2,2,2,2,2,3,3,1,1,2,3

A

Number of Houses	Frequency
1	7
2	6
3	3
4	1

C

Number of Houses	Frequency
0	0
1	3
2	5
3	7

B

Number of Houses	Frequency
1	1
2	3
3	6
4	7

D

Numbers of Houses	Frequency
2	1
4	1
6	1
5	1

GO ON

Practice Exercise 16 (cont.)

Directions: Read and solve each problem carefully. Record the correct answer on your answer sheet.

---

4 Which fraction equivalence below is true?

F $\frac{3}{4} = \frac{6}{12}$

G $\frac{2}{3} = \frac{5}{9}$

H $\frac{3}{5} = \frac{9}{15}$

J $\frac{3}{4} = \frac{9}{8}$

---

5 At a recent holiday party, there were two pies of the same size: a blueberry pie and an apple pie. The models below represent the pies, with the shaded section representing the amount eaten.

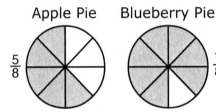

Apple Pie   Blueberry Pie

$\frac{5}{8}$ $\frac{7}{8}$

Which number below represents the total amount of pie consumed at the party?

A $\frac{12}{16}$

B $1\frac{4}{8}$

C $\frac{4}{8}$

D 2

---

6 Quinn recently made the model below to represent how much she has grown in the last year. Quinn grew 2.4 centimeters.

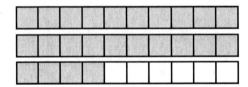

Which number below shows another way to write 2.4 centimeters?

F 204

G $\frac{204}{10}$

H $2\frac{4}{100}$

J $2\frac{4}{10}$

GO ON

Practice Exercise 16 (cont.)

Directions: Read and solve each problem carefully. Record the correct answer on your answer sheet.

7 The visual model below can be used to compare two decimals.

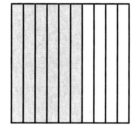 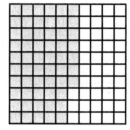

Which decimal comparison below is accurately shown by the model?

A 57 > 6

B 0.6 > 0.57

C 0.6 < 0.57

D 6 > 57

---

8 Choose the comparison below that is **NOT** true.

F $\frac{7}{8} > \frac{3}{5}$

G $\frac{3}{4} < \frac{11}{12}$

H $\frac{3}{4} < \frac{2}{3}$

J $\frac{9}{10} < \frac{11}{12}$

GO ON

Practice Exercise 16 *(cont.)*

Directions: Read and solve each problem carefully. Record the correct answer on your answer sheet.

9   Which number is a good estimate of the angle below?

   A 15º

   B 145º

   C 90º

   D 180º

---

10   What is the quotient of 435 ÷ 5? Fill in the correct bubbles on the answer sheet to record your answer.

STOP

Practice Exercise 17

Directions: Read and solve each problem carefully. Record the correct answer on your answer sheet.

1   Students in Mr. Fairfax's class recently took a math quiz. The students' scores are shown below.

> 66, 67, 68, 69, 71, 77, 79, 83, 83, 83, 83, 84, 84, 84, 88, 92, 98, 98

> 4|2 means 42.

Which stem and leaf plot accurately displays the quiz scores?

A

Stem	Leaf
4	
5	
6	6 7 8 9
7	1 7 9
8	3 4 8
9	2 8

C

Stem	Leaf
4	2
5	
6	6
7	8 9
8	3 3 3 4 4 8
9	2 9

B

Stem	Leaf
4	
5	
6	6 7 8 9
7	1 7 9
8	3 3 3 3 4 4 4 8
9	2 8 8

D

Stem	Leaf
4	
5	
6	6 7 8 9
7	1 7 9
8	3 3 4 4 8
9	1 3

2   Veronica went shopping for back-to-school supplies. The details of the items she purchased at the store are shown below.

> - 3 notebooks for $1.25 each
> - 5 highlighters for $0.25 each
> - One pack of mechanical pencils for $4.75

If Veronica gave the cashier $20.00 to pay for the items, how much change did she receive?

F $0.25

G $11.25

H $10.25

J $10.00

GO ON

Practice Exercise 17 *(cont.)*

Directions: Read and solve each problem carefully. Record the correct answer on your answer sheet.

3   What sum would have a value greater than 1?

   A $\frac{1}{4} + \frac{1}{4}$

   B $\frac{1}{4} + \frac{1}{2}$

   C $\frac{1}{3} + \frac{1}{3}$

   D $\frac{3}{4} + \frac{3}{4}$

---

4   Which choice shows the number below written in expanded form?

| 468.95 |

   F $400 + 60 + 8 + 0.9 + 0.05$ **H** $400 + 60 + 8 + 90 + 5$

   G $400 + 68 + 0.95$ **J** $400 + 60 + 8 + 0.95$

---

5   Two rectangles are shown below. What is the difference between the areas of the two rectangles?

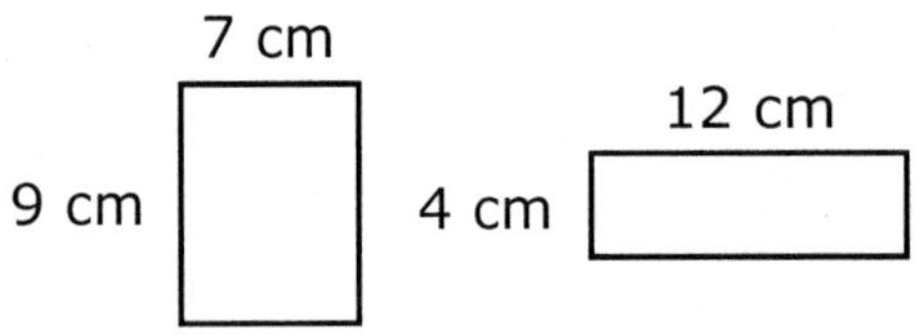

7 cm

12 cm

9 cm

4 cm

   A   48 square centimeters

   B   111 square centimeters

   C   63 square centimeters

   D   15 square centimeters

GO ON

Name: _____ Date: _____

Practice Exercise 17 (cont.)

Directions: Read and solve each problem carefully. Record the correct answer on your answer sheet.

6 An angle is shown on the protractor below.

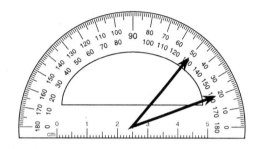

Which choice most accurately describes the measure of the angle in degrees?

F 50º   **H** 20º

G 30º   **J** 120º

---

7 An input-output tube and accompanying table are shown.

Input

Output

Position	Input	Output
1	1	1
2	4	2
3	9	3
4	16	4

Which of the following accurately describes what happens to a number when it enters the tube?

A It is multiplied by 2.

B It is divided by 2.

C It is divided by the position number.

D It is multiplied by the position number.

GO ON ▶

Practice Exercise 17 *(cont.)*

Directions: Read and solve each problem carefully. Record the correct answer on your answer sheet.

---

8 How many lines of symmetry does the shape below have?

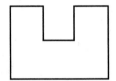

F 0

G 1

H 2

J 3

---

9 The fraction $\frac{7}{10}$ can be represented by the expression below.

$$\frac{1}{10} + \frac{1}{10} + \frac{1}{10} + \boxed{} + \frac{1}{10} + \frac{1}{10} + \frac{1}{10}$$

Which number goes in $\boxed{}$ to make the equation true?

A $\frac{1}{10}$

B $\frac{7}{10}$

C $\frac{6}{60}$

D $\frac{1}{60}$

---

10 A number line is shown below. What decimal represents point *R* on the number line? Fill in the correct bubbles on the answer sheet to record your answer.

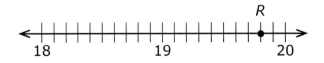

STOP

Practice Exercise 18

Directions: Read and solve each problem carefully. Record the correct answer on your answer sheet.

1   Janelle is training for a marathon. She recently completed a training run that was 19.05 miles. Which of the numbers below is another way to express this distance?

   A $19\frac{5}{10}$

   B $19\frac{5}{100}$

   C 1,905

   D $20\frac{5}{10}$

---

2   On a shopping spree, Erica spent $639.97. Erica had $750.00 before the shopping spree. How much money does she have now?

   F $110.03

   G $1,389.97

   H $110.97

   J $111.03

---

3   There are 3,482 people waiting in line for a ski lift. If 3 people can fit on each chair, how many chairs are needed to get everyone to the top?

   A 1,162

   B 1,160

   C 1,161

   D 10,446

GO ON

Practice Exercise 18 (cont.)

Directions: Read and solve each problem carefully. Record the correct answer on your answer sheet.

4   Janelle received a great deal of money for her birthday. Rather than spend the money, she wants to keep it safe for later use. Which of the following actions should she take with her money in order to keep it safest?

   F Put it in a financial institution

   G Hide it under her bed

   H Ask a responsible friend to hold onto the money until Janelle needs it

   J Put it into a piggy bank

5   The shape below has a variety of angle sizes.

   Which choice correctly names the number of acute angles in the entire shape?

   A 1   **C** 3

   B 2   **D** 4

6   Which unit would be best for measuring the amount of water the pool below could hold?

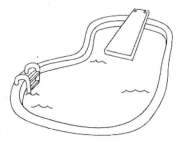

   F Cups   **H** Quarts

   G Pints   **J** Gallons

GO ON

Practice Exercise 18 (cont.)

Directions: Read and solve each problem carefully. Record the correct answer on your answer sheet.

7 Aiden bought 15 packs of 24 bottles of water for a road race. To make them easy to carry, he is packaging 4 bottles in a bag. Which equation can be used to determine b, the number of bags Aiden will fill?

A $15 \times 24 = b$

B $b = 15 + 24 + 4$

C $15 = (b \times 24) \div 4$

D $(15 \times 24) \div 4 = b$

---

8 Which statement about the number below is true?

$$32,255$$

F The fives have the same value.

G The five in the tens place is worth 100 times as much as the five in the ones place.

H The five in the tens place is worth 1,000 times as much as the five in the ones place.

J The five in the ones place is worth $\frac{1}{10}$ as much as the five in the tens place.

GO ON

Practice Exercise 18 *(cont.)*

Directions: Read and solve each problem carefully. Record the correct answer on your answer sheet.

9   Fraction comparisons are shown below. Which comparison is **NOT** true?

   A $\frac{4}{5} > \frac{3}{4}$

   B $\frac{2}{3} < \frac{7}{8}$

   C $\frac{1}{2} = \frac{6}{12}$

   D $\frac{3}{4} > \frac{5}{6}$

---

10   What is the product of 45×10 ? Fill in the correct bubbles on the answer sheet to record your answer.

STOP

Practice Exercise 19

Directions: Read and solve each problem carefully. Record the correct answer on your answer sheet.

1 What addition problem is represented by the number line below?

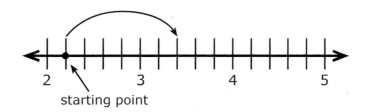

starting point

A $2\frac{1}{5} + 1\frac{1}{5}$

B $2\frac{1}{5} + 3\frac{2}{5}$

C $2\frac{2}{5} + \frac{6}{5}$

D $0 + 3\frac{2}{5}$

---

2 Use the image below to determine the measure of angle *WYZ*.

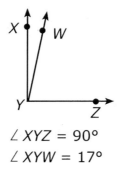

$\angle XYZ = 90°$

$\angle XYW = 17°$

F 73°

G 70°

H 90°

J 45°

GO ON

Practice Exercise 19 *(cont.)*

Directions: Read and solve each problem carefully. Record the correct answer on your answer sheet.

3 Daniel is training for a running race. For weeks, he kept track of the distances he ran each day. This data is shown on the dot plot below.

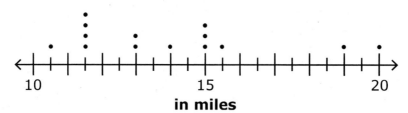

Distances Run

in miles

Which list correctly names Daniel's running distances?

A $11\frac{1}{2}$, $11\frac{1}{2}$, $11\frac{1}{2}$, $11\frac{1}{2}$

B 10, $10\frac{1}{2}$, 11, $11\frac{1}{2}$, 12, $12\frac{1}{2}$, 13, $13\frac{1}{2}$, 14, 15, 16, 17, 18, 19, 20

C $10\frac{1}{2}$, $11\frac{1}{2}$, 13, 14, 15, $15\frac{1}{2}$, 19, 20

D $10\frac{1}{2}$, $11\frac{1}{2}$, $11\frac{1}{2}$, $11\frac{1}{2}$, $11\frac{1}{2}$, 13, 13, 14, 15, 15, 15, $15\frac{1}{2}$, 19, 20

---

4 Alison saved $264 to buy a new car. The car costs 100 times what Alison has saved. What is the cost of the car?

F $2,640

G $26,400

H $464

J $27,400

---

5 Sammy weighed 55 pounds at his doctor's appointment last year. When Sammy went to his doctor's appointment this year, he weighed 64 pounds. How much weight did Sammy gain in ounces?

A 160 ounces

B 9 ounces

C 16 ounces

D 144 ounces

GO ON

Practice Exercise 19 *(cont.)*

Directions: Read and solve each problem carefully. Record the correct answer on your answer sheet.

6 The number below has a digit underlined.

$$3,8\underline{7}4,912.45$$

What is the value of this digit?

F 7,000,000

G 70,000

H 7

J 70

7 What is the perimeter of the rectangle shown?

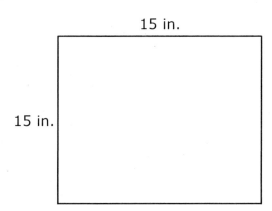

15 in.

15 in.

A 60 inches

B 180 inches

C 27 inches

D 144 inches

GO ON

Practice Exercise 19 *(cont.)*

Directions: Read and solve each problem carefully. Record the correct answer on your answer sheet.

8   Which choice below shows an example of perpendicular lines?

F

H

G

J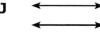

---

9   Round the numbers in the expression below to the nearest hundred to estimate the difference.

$$4{,}365 - 2{,}608$$

A 1,000

B 2,000

C 300

D 1,800

---

10   Find the product of 35 and 28. Fill in the correct bubbles on the answer sheet to record your answer.

STOP

Practice Exercise 20

Directions: Read and solve each problem carefully. Record the correct answer on your answer sheet.

1 Which of the input-output tables below follows the rule "multiply by three, and then subtract 2"?

A

In	Out
1	6
2	12
3	18
4	24

C

In	Out
1	3
2	6
3	9
4	12

B

In	Out
2	8
4	14
6	20
8	26

D

In	Out
3	7
6	16
9	25
12	34

---

2 Paul is on a road trip and has to travel a total distance of 1,543.4 miles. If he has traveled 432 miles so far, how many miles does he have remaining?

F 1,111 miles

G 1,111.4 miles

H 1,111.6 miles

J 1,975.4 miles

---

3 A division problem can be represented using the model below where the dividend is inside the rectangle. One dimension is the divisor and the other is the quotient. Use the model to find the other dimension.

6 | 648

A 4,104

B 108

C 112

D 116

GO ON

Practice Exercise 20 *(cont.)*

Directions: Read and solve each problem carefully. Record the correct answer on your answer sheet.

4   Two protractors are shown below.

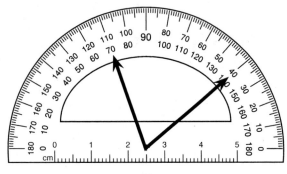   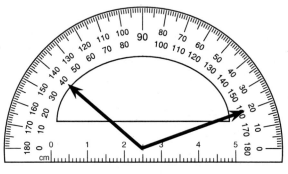

Protractor *A*   Protractor *B*

Which protractor shows an angle that is closest to 70 degrees?

F   Protractor *A*

G   Protractor *B*

H   Both protractors show an angle that appears to equal 70 degrees.

J   Neither protractor shows an angle of 70 degrees.

---

5   Alexandria's car can drive 26 miles on each gallon of gas. If her gas tank can hold 14 gallons of gas, how many miles can she drive?

A   200   **C**   40

B   218   **D**   364

---

6   What number can be represented by the model below?

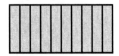      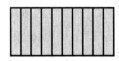   

F   300.3   **H**   3.3

G   30.3   **J**   3.03

GO ON ➡

Practice Exercise 20 *(cont.)*

Directions: Read and solve each problem carefully. Record the correct answer on your answer sheet.

7   Which comparison below is true?

  A $\frac{5}{10} > \frac{7}{12}$

  B $\frac{6}{12} < \frac{3}{5}$

  C $\frac{3}{4} > \frac{7}{8}$

  D $\frac{2}{3} < \frac{1}{2}$

---

8   Tina went to a yard sale and bought 4 chairs for $20.00 each. She went home, sanded and painted the chairs, and then sold them for $35.00 each. Assuming she had the sandpaper and paint (and therefore didn't spend money on them), how much profit did Tina make from selling all 4 chairs?

  F $15.00

  G $55.00

  H $60.00

  J $220.00

GO ON

Practice Exercise 20 *(cont.)*

Directions: Read and solve each problem carefully. Record the correct answer on your answer sheet.

9   A fraction equation is shown below.

$$\frac{3}{10} + \frac{3}{10} + \frac{3}{10} = \frac{9}{10}$$

What is another way the fraction $\frac{9}{10}$ could be decomposed?

A $\frac{4}{10} + \frac{6}{10}$

B $\frac{4}{10} + \frac{2}{10} + \frac{2}{10} + \frac{1}{10}$

C $\frac{2}{10} + \frac{5}{10} + \frac{3}{10}$

D $\frac{1}{10} + \frac{1}{10} + \frac{1}{10} + \frac{5}{10}$

---

10   What is $34\frac{17}{100}$ written as a decimal? Fill in the correct bubbles on the answer sheet to record your answer.

STOP

Practice Exercise 21

Directions: Read and solve each problem carefully. Record the correct answer on your answer sheet.

1   Which statement about the number 324,986.51 is true?

    A   The digit 6 has a value of (6 × 100).

    B   The digit 6 has a value of (6 × 10).

    C   The digit 2 has a value of (2 × 10,000).

    D   The digit 3 has a value of (300,000 × 3).

---

2   Jennifer argued that the sum of $\frac{3}{4}$ and $\frac{3}{4}$ must be greater than 2, since 3 + 3 = 6. Lindsey thinks the sum is less than 2, because both fractions are less than 2. Which person is correct?

    F   Lindsey is correct.

    G   Jennifer is correct.

    H   Neither girl is correct, because the sum is less than 1.

    J   Neither girl is correct, because the sum is exactly 2.

---

3   The representation below is being used to model the addition of $\frac{6}{15}$ (solid circles) and $\frac{5}{15}$ (dotted circles). What is the sum of these two fractions?

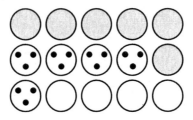

    A $\frac{4}{15}$ **C** $\frac{22}{30}$

    B $\frac{11}{15}$ **D** $\frac{11}{11}$

GO ON ➤

Practice Exercise 21 *(cont.)*

Directions: Read and solve each problem carefully. Record the correct answer on your answer sheet.

4 Which shape below has no right angles?

F

G

H

J

---

5 Maria scored 12 regular baskets (worth 2 points each) and 7 three-pointers during a recent basketball game. If Maria scored an equivalent number of points in the next 2 games, what would be her point total for all 3 games?

A 57 points

B 45 points

C 90 points

D 135 points

---

6 Use the model below to answer the question.

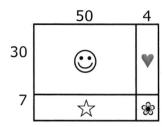

What expression can be used to find the area of the rectangle marked with the star?

F 54 × 37

G 4 × 7

H 50 × 7

J 50 × 37

GO ON ➡

Practice Exercise 21 *(cont.)*

Directions: Read and solve each problem carefully. Record the correct answer on your answer sheet.

7 The frequency table below shows the rainfall in centimeters for each day in April.

Rainfall (cm) on Each April Day	Frequency
$0-\frac{1}{4}$ cm	16
$\frac{1}{2}$ cm $-\frac{3}{4}$ cm	10
1cm $-1\frac{1}{4}$ cm	1
$1\frac{1}{2}-1\frac{3}{4}$ cm	2
$2-2\frac{1}{4}$ cm	1

Which data set below matches the first row of data in the frequency table?

A 1, 1, 2, 10, 16

B 0, 0, 0, 0, 0, 0, 0, 0, 0, 0, $\frac{1}{4}$, $\frac{1}{4}$, $\frac{1}{4}$, $\frac{1}{4}$, $\frac{1}{4}$, $\frac{1}{4}$

C $\frac{1}{2}$, $\frac{1}{2}$, $\frac{1}{2}$, $\frac{1}{2}$, $\frac{1}{2}$, $\frac{1}{2}$, $\frac{1}{2}$, $\frac{1}{2}$, $\frac{1}{2}$, $\frac{1}{2}$

D 1, $1\frac{1}{2}$, $1\frac{1}{2}$, $2\frac{1}{4}$

---

8 The distance from school to Jamal's house is 75 yards. What would the distance be if Jamal were to measure the distance in inches?

F 225 inches

G 2,700 inches

H 900 inches

J 111 inches

GO ON

Name: _____   Date: _____

Practice Exercise 21 *(cont.)*

Directions: Read and solve each problem carefully. Record the correct answer on your answer sheet.

9   Which of the triangles below is **not** an acute triangle?

A

B

C

D

---

10   What number is worth $\frac{1}{10}$ as much as the underlined digit in 34,9<u>8</u>7? Fill in the correct bubbles on the answer sheet to record your answer.

STOP

Name: _____   Date: _____

Practice Exercise 22

Directions: Read and solve each problem carefully. Record the correct answer on your answer sheet.

1 What is the measure in degrees of the angle shown on the protractor below?

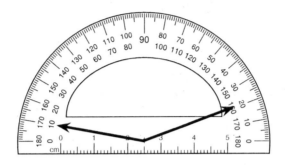

A 180º

B 170º

C 30º

D 150º

---

2 Look at the input-output table below:

Position	Input	Output
1	2	8
2	3	12
3	4	16
4	5	20

How is a number's position related to the output?

F Add one to position and multiply by 5.

G Add one to position and multiply by 4.

H Add two to position and multiply by 2.

J Multiply position by 8.

Practice Exercise 22 *(cont.)*

Directions: Read and solve each problem carefully. Record the correct answer on your answer sheet.

3 Two rectangles are positioned side by side. One rectangle is 4-by-7 inches, the other is 6-by-5 inches. What is the difference in square inches in the areas of the rectangles?

A 30 square inches

B 28 square inches

C 2 square inches

D 58 square inches

4 Which shape named below has exactly two sets of parallel lines?

F Trapezoid

G Parallelogram

H Acute triangle

J Regular hexagon

5 What is the difference for the expression below?

$$32{,}985 - 28{,}023.43$$

A 4,961.57

B 4,961.43

C 4,962.43

D 61,008.43

GO ON

Practice Exercise 22 *(cont.)*

Directions: Read and solve each problem carefully. Record the correct answer on your answer sheet.

6 Adam baked 2 pans of brownies for a party. He cut each tray into 12 pieces as represented by the model below.

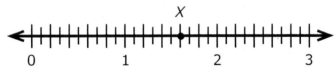

If a total of 15 brownies was eaten, what expression below would give the fraction of brownies remaining?

F $2 + 1\frac{3}{12}$

G $2 - \frac{9}{30}$

H $2 - \frac{9}{15}$

J $2 - 1\frac{3}{12}$

---

7 Which number below represents point *X* on the number line?

X

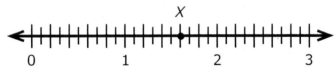

| 0 | 1 | 2 | 3 |

A 1   **C** 1.6

B 2   **D** 1.06

---

8 Which digit can replace the blank space to make the comparison true?

$$34,198,026 > 34,\_98,026$$

F 3

G 2

H 1

J 0

GO ON ➡

Name: _____ Date: _____

Practice Exercise 22 *(cont.)*

Directions: Read and solve each problem carefully. Record the correct answer on your answer sheet.

9 Use the models below to answer the question.

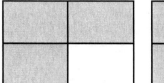 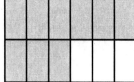

Which statement correctly describes the relationship between the two fractions shown?

A The fractions are not equivalent. One has three parts missing and the other has one.

B The fractions are not equivalent. They each have a different number of parts shaded.

C The fractions are equivalent. Even though they are broken into different amounts, the portion of each shaded area is the same.

D The fractions cannot be compared because they are not cut into the same number of parts.

---

10 At a crayon packaging facility, each box can hold 12 crayons. If the machine makes 149 crayons, how many boxes can be filled? Fill in the correct bubbles on the answer sheet to record your answer.

Name: _____ Date: _____

Practice Exercise 23

Directions: Read and solve each problem carefully. Record the correct answer on your answer sheet.

1 Michael is taking a road trip, and needs to travel 4,320 miles over the course of 10 days. If he wants to drive an equal number of miles, m, each day, which equation below could he use to determine the daily distance?

    A $4,320 - 10 = m$

    B $4,320 \div m = m$

    C $4,320 \div 10 = m$

    D $4,320 \times 10 = m$

---

2 Which angle below appears to measure 20 degrees?

F

G

H

J

---

3 Sarah has $3,245.23 in her bank account. She deposits another $234.43. What is Sarah's new balance in her account?

    A $3,479.66

    B $5,479.66

    C $3,010.80

    D $5,058.95

GO ON

Practice Exercise 23 *(cont.)*

Directions: Read and solve each problem carefully. Record the correct answer on your answer sheet.

4   Olivia is purchasing a house and she needs to borrow money. Which of the choices below would be the safest place from which Olivia could borrow the money?

F   A close friend   **H**   Her dad

G   A financial institution   **J**   Her sister

---

5   Use the frequency table below to answer the question.

Tracking Storms in the Pacific Northwest

Month	# of Storms
January	25
February	12
March	23
April	34
May	64
June	94
July	209
August	301
September	265
October	215
November	134
December	67

How many total storms occurred from August through October?

A 516   **C** 771

B 566   **D** 781

GO ON

Practice Exercise 23 *(cont.)*

Directions: Read and solve each problem carefully. Record the correct answer on your answer sheet.

6   Which shape shown below does **NOT** have obtuse angles?

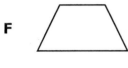

F

G

H

J

---

7   The stem and leaf plot below represents the ages of students enrolled in a local computer course.

Stem	Leaf
1	4 6 6 7
2	8
3	7 9
4	2 5 6 7 9

1|4 means 14.

Which data set below matches the data displayed on the stem and leaf plot?

A   14, 16, 17, 28, 37, 39, 42, 45, 46, 47, 49

B   14, 16, 16, 17, 28, 37, 39, 42, 45, 46, 47, 49

C   14, 28, 37, 39, 42, 45, 46, 47, 49

D   46, 67, 28, 79, 25, 67, 79

---

8   Which of the numbers below matches 6.98?

F $6\frac{98}{100}$

G 698

H $6\frac{89}{100}$

J $\frac{698}{1000}$

GO ON

Practice Exercise 23 *(cont.)*

Directions: Read and solve each problem carefully. Record the correct answer on your answer sheet.

9 Which symbol should be entered in the box to make the comparison below true?

$$\frac{7}{8} \ \square \ \frac{11}{12}$$

A >

B <

C =

D o

---

10 Tyler bought 9 large bags of candy. Each large bag had 126 pieces of candy. Tyler is going to put three pieces in smaller bags to pass out at Halloween. How many small bags can Tyler make? Fill in the correct bubbles on the answer sheet to record your answer.

STOP

Name: _____ Date: _____

Practice Exercise 24

Directions: Read and solve each problem carefully. Record the correct answer on your answer sheet.

1 Use the number line to determine the sum of the fractions below.

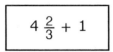 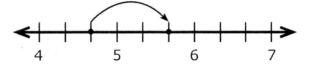

$4\frac{2}{3} + 1$

A 5

C 6

B $5\frac{1}{3}$

D $5\frac{2}{3}$

---

2 An input-output machine is shown below.

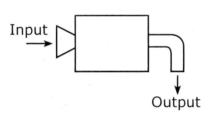

Input	Output
10	25
11	28
12	31
13	34
14	37

Which of the following could be the rule applied to the inputs as they pass through the machine to produce the outputs?

F Multiply by 25

H Multiply by 3, subtract 5

G Multiply by 4, subtract 15

J Multiply by 5, subtract 25

---

3 Which of the following shows how to accurately decompose the fraction $\frac{7}{5}$ into unit fractions?

A $\frac{1}{5} + 1 + 1 + 1 + 1 + 1 + 1$

B $\frac{1}{5} + 6$

C $\frac{1}{5} + \frac{1}{5} + \frac{1}{5} + \frac{1}{5} + \frac{1}{5} + \frac{1}{5} + \frac{1}{5}$

D $\frac{1}{5} + \frac{1}{5} + 5$

GO ON

Practice Exercise 24 (cont.)

Directions: Read and solve each problem carefully. Record the correct answer on your answer sheet.

4   Use the models to put the decimals into order from least to greatest

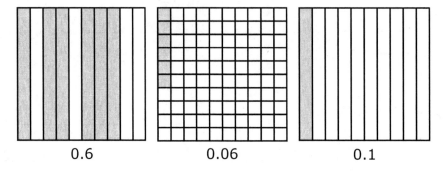

0.6	0.06	0.1

   F   0.1, 0.06, 0.6

   G   0.06, 0.1, 0.6

   H   0.6, 0.1, 0.06

   J   0.1, 0.6, 0.06

---

5   Jamie bought bananas that cost $0.50 a pound. If he bought 9 pounds of bananas and paid with $10.00, which equation represents *c*, the change he will receive?

   A $0.50 × 9 = c

   B   c × $0.50 = 9

   C $10.00 − ($0.50 × 9) = c

   D   c + $10.00 = $0.50 × 9

---

6   Which equation shows 80,502.07 written in expanded form?

   F   80,000 + 502 + 0.07

   G   80,000 + 500 + 2 + 0.07

   H   8,000 + 500 + 2

   J   80 + 500 + 2 + 0.07

GO ON

Name: _____ Date: _____

Practice Exercise 24 *(cont.)*

Directions: Read and solve each problem carefully. Record the correct answer on your answer sheet.

7   Carmichael left his house at 5:15 A.M. He returned at 6:25 P.M. How long was Carmichael gone?

   A 1 hour, 10 minutes

   B 11 hours, 10 minutes

   C 10 hours, 10 minutes

   D 13 hours, 10 minutes

---

8   How many lines of symmetry does the figure below have?

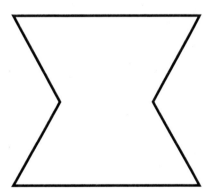

   F 0

   G 1

   H 2

   J 3

GO ON

Practice Exercise 24 *(cont.)*

Directions: Read and solve each problem carefully. Record the correct answer on your answer sheet.

9   What is the quotient of 4,956 divided by 6?

   A 4,950

   B 826

   C 29,736

   D 726

---

10   What is the measure of the angle shown on the protractor below? Fill in the correct bubbles on the answer sheet to record your answer.

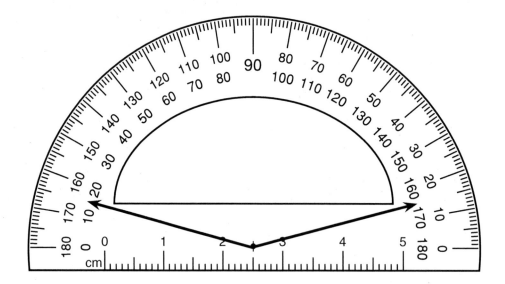

Practice Exercise 25

Directions: Read and solve each problem carefully. Record the correct answer on your answer sheet.

1 A container of orange juice holds 32 ounces. If Jennifer bought 24 containers for an upcoming brunch, how many 8 ounce servings can she make?

    A 96

    B 768

    C 64

    D 6,144

---

2 Sharon kayaked for 25.31 miles. What is another way to express this distance?

    F 25.031 mi

    G $25\frac{31}{100}$ mi

    H 2,531 mi

    J $\frac{25}{31}$ mi

---

3 This stem and leaf plot shows a group of students' scores on a recent exam.

Stem	Leaf
7	7 8 9 9
8	1 2 4 4 7 7 8 8
9	5 5 5 6 7
10	0

7|7 means 77.

Which of the following data sets matches the data from the stem and leaf plot?

    A 78, 79, 12, 14, 14, 17, 17, 18, 18, 55, 56, 70

    B 77, 78, 79, 81, 82, 84, 87, 88, 95, 96, 97, 100

    C 77, 78, 79, 79, 81, 82, 84, 84, 87, 87, 88, 88, 95, 95, 95, 96, 97, 100

    D 77, 78, 79, 79, 81, 82, 84, 84, 87, 88, 95, 95, 96, 97, 100

GO ON

Practice Exercise 25 (cont.)

Directions: Read and solve each problem carefully. Record the correct answer on your answer sheet.

4 Fiona has different expenses she has to pay each month. Only one of the expenses is fixed while the rest are variable. Choose the expense that is most likely a fixed expense.

F Mortgage

G Heat

H Hot water

J Electricity

---

5 What is the difference of 4,502.98 – 324.20?

A 1,260.98

B 4,827.18

C 417,878

D 4,178.78

---

6 What is the area of the rectangle below?

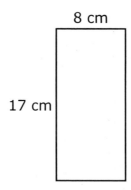

8 cm

17 cm

F 25 square centimeters

G 50 square centimeters

H 136 square centimeters

J 95 square centimeters

GO ON

Practice Exercise 25 *(cont.)*

Directions: Read and solve each problem carefully. Record the correct answer on your answer sheet.

Take a Safari

Animal	Features	Average Male Size	Food	Did You Know?
Plains zebra	black and white stripes; manes of short stiff hairs	four to five feet tall; 550 pounds	grass, leaves, bark, roots, stems, and shrubs	It has excellent vision and hearing.
Black rhinoceros	gray, thick, hairless skin; two horns; hooked upper lip	four to six feet tall; 3,000 pounds	twigs, leaves, grass, bushes, and shrubs	It is nearsighted (cannot see objects that are far away).
Giraffe	tan, patterned coat; long neck; short horns	15 to 19 feet tall; 2,200 pounds	leaves, flowers, and fruit	It is the tallest animal on Earth.
African elephant	sloping back; rounded, large ears; ivory tusks; trunk with two lips	10 to 13 feet tall; 11,000 pounds	grass, bark, shrubs, and fruit	Its ivory tusks are very long teeth.
Hippopotamus	thick, hairless body; ears, nostrils and eyes on top of head	four to five feet tall; 4,400 pounds	short grass	It can stay under water for five minutes.

Source: *TIME For Kids*

7 About how many pounds would 4 black rhinos weigh?

   A 3,000   **C** 9,000

   B 6,000   **D** 12,000

8 What is the combined average weight of the two tallest animals?

   F 11,550 pounds   **H** 14,000 pounds

   G 13,200 pounds   **J** 15,400 pounds

GO ON

Practice Exercise 25 *(cont.)*

Directions: Read and solve each problem carefully. Record the correct answer on your answer sheet.

9 Which of the input-output tables below follows the rule "add three, and then multiply by 6"?

A

Input	Output
3	6
6	9
9	12
12	15

C

Input	Output
2	30
3	36
4	42
5	48

B

Input	Output
1	4
2	7
3	10
4	13

D

Input	Output
2	12
3	18
4	24
5	36

10 Estimate the difference by rounding each of the numbers in the subtraction expression to the nearest 10.

$$856 - 489$$

Fill in the correct bubbles on the answer sheet to record your answer.

STOP

Name: _____   Date: _____

Answer Sheet

Practice Exercise _____

Directions: Fill in each correct answer.

1 Ⓐ Ⓑ Ⓒ Ⓓ
2 Ⓕ Ⓖ Ⓗ Ⓙ
3 Ⓐ Ⓑ Ⓒ Ⓓ
4 Ⓕ Ⓖ Ⓗ Ⓙ
5 Ⓐ Ⓑ Ⓒ Ⓓ
6 Ⓕ Ⓖ Ⓗ Ⓙ
7 Ⓐ Ⓑ Ⓒ Ⓓ
8 Ⓕ Ⓖ Ⓗ Ⓙ
9 Ⓐ Ⓑ Ⓒ Ⓓ

10

			.		
①	①	①		①	①
②	②	②		②	②
③	③	③		③	③
④	④	④		④	④
⑤	⑤	⑤		⑤	⑤
⑥	⑥	⑥		⑥	⑥
⑦	⑦	⑦		⑦	⑦
⑧	⑧	⑧		⑧	⑧
⑨	⑨	⑨		⑨	⑨

- -

Name: _____   Date: _____

Answer Sheet

Practice Exercise _____

Directions: Fill in each correct answer.

1 Ⓐ Ⓑ Ⓒ Ⓓ
2 Ⓕ Ⓖ Ⓗ Ⓙ
3 Ⓐ Ⓑ Ⓒ Ⓓ
4 Ⓕ Ⓖ Ⓗ Ⓙ
5 Ⓐ Ⓑ Ⓒ Ⓓ
6 Ⓕ Ⓖ Ⓗ Ⓙ
7 Ⓐ Ⓑ Ⓒ Ⓓ
8 Ⓕ Ⓖ Ⓗ Ⓙ
9 Ⓐ Ⓑ Ⓒ Ⓓ

10

			.		
①	①	①		①	①
②	②	②		②	②
③	③	③		③	③
④	④	④		④	④
⑤	⑤	⑤		⑤	⑤
⑥	⑥	⑥		⑥	⑥
⑦	⑦	⑦		⑦	⑦
⑧	⑧	⑧		⑧	⑧
⑨	⑨	⑨		⑨	⑨

References Cited

Texas Education Agency. 2014. *State of Texas Assessment of Academic Readiness: A Parent's Guide to the Student Testing Program.* TEA: Texas.

Correlation to Assessed Standards

The following chart correlates each question in this book to its designated eligible TEKS.

	Item Number	Reporting Category	Content Student Expectation	Readiness or Supporting
Practice Exercise 1	1	1	4.2.G	Readiness
	2	2	4.4.H	Readiness
	3	1	4.2.C	Supporting
	4	3	4.8.C	Readiness
	5	1	4.3.D	Readiness
	6	2	4.4.F	Supporting
	7	2	4.4.A	Readiness
	8	3	4.6.D	Readiness
	9	1	4.2.A	Supporting
	10	2	4.4.D	Supporting
Practice Exercise 2	1	1	4.2.D	Supporting
	2	1	4.2.B	Readiness
	3	4	4.9.A	Readiness
	4	3	4.5.D	Readiness
	5	1	4.3.C	Supporting
	6	3	4.7.C	Readiness
	7	2	4.5.A	Readiness
	8	2	4.4.B	Supporting
	9	1	4.2.H	Supporting
	10	3	4.8.C	Readiness
Practice Exercise 3	1	2	4.3.E	Readiness
	2	2	4.5.B	Readiness
	3	3	4.6.B	Supporting
	4	2	4.4.H	Readiness
	5	3	4.5.D	Readiness
	6	1	4.3.B	Supporting
	7	4	4.9.A	Readiness
	8	1	4.2.G	Readiness
	9	1	4.2.F	Supporting
	10	2	4.4.A	Readiness

	Item Number	Reporting Category	Content Student Expectation	Readiness or Supporting
Practice Exercise 4	1	2	4.4.E	Supporting
	2	2	4.5.A	Readiness
	3	1	4.3.D	Readiness
	4	1	4.2.B	Readiness
	5	3	4.6.A	Supporting
	6	2	4.5.B	Readiness
	7	3	4.6.D	Readiness
	8	3	4.7.C	Readiness
	9	2	4.3.F	Supporting
	10	3	4.8.C	Readiness
Practice Exercise 5	1	1	4.2.G	Readiness
	2	2	4.3.E	Readiness
	3	3	4.7.D	Supporting
	4	3	4.5.D	Readiness
	5	2	4.4.A	Readiness
	6	2	4.4.G	Supporting
	7	2	4.4.H	Readiness
	8	4	4.9.A	Readiness
	9	4	4.10.B	Supporting
	10	2	4.5.A	Readiness
Practice Exercise 6	1	1	4.2.E	Supporting
	2	1	4.2.G	Readiness
	3	3	4.6.D	Readiness
	4	1	4.2.B	Readiness
	5	3	4.7.E	Supporting
	6	2	4.5.B	Readiness
	7	2	4.3.E	Readiness
	8	2	4.3.E	Readiness
	9	2	4.3.E	Supporting
	10	3	4.8.C	Readiness

Correlation to Assessed Standards (cont.)

	Item Number	Reporting Category	Content Student Expectation	Readiness or Supporting
Practice Exercise 7	1	2	4.3.E	Readiness
	2	2	4.4.H	Readiness
	3	4	4.10.A	Supporting
	4	2	4.5.A	Readiness
	5	3	4.6.A	Supporting
	6	4	4.9.A	Readiness
	7	3	4.5.D	Readiness
	8	3	4.8.B	Supporting
	9	2	4.4.C	Supporting
	10	3	4.8.C	Readiness
Practice Exercise 8	1	3	4.7.C	Readiness
	2	3	4.8.C	Readiness
	3	3	4.6.D	Readiness
	4	3	4.6.C	Supporting
	5	1	4.3.A	Supporting
	6	1	4.3.D	Readiness
	7	1	4.2.G	Readiness
	8	1	4.2.D	Supporting
	9	1	4.2.B	Readiness
	10	3	4.5.D	Readiness
Practice Exercise 9	1	2	4.4.A	Readiness
	2	1	4.3.G	Supporting
	3	2	4.3.E	Readiness
	4	1	4.2.B	Readiness
	5	2	4.5.A	Readiness
	6	4	4.10.E	Supporting
	7	4	4.9.B	Supporting
	8	3	4.6.D	Readiness
	9	2	4.5.B	Readiness
	10	2	4.4.H	Readiness

	Item Number	Reporting Category	Content Student Expectation	Readiness or Supporting
Practice Exercise 10	1	1	4.2.G	Readiness
	2	3	4.5.D	Readiness
	3	1	4.3.D	Readiness
	4	4	4.10.B	Supporting
	5	3	4.8.C	Readiness
	6	3	4.6.B	Supporting
	7	4	4.9.A	Readiness
	8	3	4.7.C	Readiness
	9	2	4.4.B	Supporting
	10	2	4.4.A	Readiness
Practice Exercise 11	1	2	4.3.E	Readiness
	2	2	4.4.H	Readiness
	3	1	4.2.D	Supporting
	4	1	4.2.B	Readiness
	5	2	4.5.A	Readiness
	6	3	4.6.D	Readiness
	7	1	4.3.D	Readiness
	8	2	4.5.B	Readiness
	9	3	4.8.C	Readiness
	10	2	4.4.F	Supporting
Practice Exercise 12	1	3	4.7.C	Readiness
	2	2	4.3.E	Readiness
	3	4	4.9.A	Readiness
	4	1	4.2.C	Supporting
	5	2	4.4.A	Readiness
	6	2	4.5.B	Readiness
	7	2	4.4.A	Readiness
	8	2	4.4.A	Readiness
	9	1	4.4.A	Supporting
	10	3	4.8.B	Supporting

51703—Time For Kids: Practicing for STAAR Success © *Shell Education*

Correlation to Assessed Standards *(cont.)*

	Item Number	Reporting Category	Content Student Expectation	Readiness or Supporting
Practice Exercise 13	1	3	4.6.D	Readiness
	2	3	4.5.D	Readiness
	3	1	4.2.H	Supporting
	4	1	4.2.B	Readiness
	5	1	4.3.D	Readiness
	6	2	4.4.C	Supporting
	7	2	4.4.H	Readiness
	8	2	4.5.A	Readiness
	9	2	4.5.B	Readiness
	10	2	4.4.G	Supporting
Practice Exercise 14	1	4	4.9.A	Readiness
	2	3	4.8.C	Readiness
	3	2	4.3.E	Readiness
	4	1	4.2.G	Readiness
	5	3	4.6.C	Supporting
	6	3	4.8.A	Supporting
	7	2	4.4.G	Supporting
	8	2	4.4.A	Readiness
	9	1	4.3.D	Readiness
	10	1	4.2.B	Readiness
Practice Exercise 15	1	3	4.5.D	Readiness
	2	1	4.2.B	Readiness
	3	4	4.10.A	Supporting
	4	3	4.8.C	Readiness
	5	2	4.5.B	Readiness
	6	2	4.4.A	Readiness
	7	2	4.4.E	Supporting
	8	3	4.7.C	Readiness
	9	3	4.8.B	Supporting
	10	3	4.7.E	Supporting

	Item Number	Reporting Category	Content Student Expectation	Readiness or Supporting
Practice Exercise 16	1	3	4.6.D	Readiness
	2	2	4.4.H	Readiness
	3	2	4.5.A	Readiness
	4	1	4.3.C	Supporting
	5	2	4.3.E	Readiness
	6	1	4.2.G	Readiness
	7	1	4.2.F	Supporting
	8	3	4.7.D	Supporting
	9	1	4.3.D	Readiness
	10	2	4.4.F	Supporting
Practice Exercise 17	1	4	4.9.A	Readiness
	2	3	4.8.C	Readiness
	3	2	4.3.F	Supporting
	4	1	4.2.B	Readiness
	5	3	4.5.D	Readiness
	6	3	4.7.C	Readiness
	7	2	4.5.B	Readiness
	8	3	4.6.B	Supporting
	9	1	4.3.A	Supporting
	10			
Practice Exercise 18	1	1	4.2.G	Readiness
	2	2	4.4.A	Readiness
	3	2	4.4.H	Readiness
	4	4	4.10.E	Supporting
	5	3	4.6.D	Readiness
	6	3	4.8.A	Supporting
	7	2	4.5.A	Readiness
	8	1	4.2.A	Supporting
	9	1	4.3.D	Readiness
	10			

Correlation to Assessed Standards *(cont.)*

	Item Number	Reporting Category	Content Student Expectation	Readiness or Supporting
Practice Exercise 19	1	2	4.3.E	Readiness
	2	3	4.7.E	Readiness
	3	4	4.9.A	Readiness
	4	2	4.4.B	Supporting
	5	3	4.8.C	Readiness
	6	1	4.2.B	Readiness
	7	3	4.5.D	Readiness
	8	3	4.6.A	Supporting
	9	2	4.4.G	Supporting
	10	2	4.4.D	Supporting
Practice Exercise 20	1	2	4.5.B	Readiness
	2	2	4.4.A	Readiness
	3	2	4.4.E	Supporting
	4	3	4.7.C	Readiness
	5	2	4.4.H	Readiness
	6	1	4.2.E	Supporting
	7	1	4.3.D	Readiness
	8	4	4.10.B	Supporting
	9	1	4.3.B	Supporting
	10	1	4.2.G	Readiness
Practice Exercise 21	1	1	4.2.B	Readiness
	2	2	4.3.F	Supporting
	3	2	4.3.E	Readiness
	4	3	4.6.D	Readiness
	5	2	4.5.A	Readiness
	6	2	4.4.C	Supporting
	7	4	4.9.A	Readiness
	8	3	4.8.C	Supporting
	9	3	4.6.C	Supporting
	10	1	4.2.A	Supporting

	Item Number	Reporting Category	Content Student Expectation	Readiness or Supporting
Practice Exercise 22	1	3	4.7.C	Readiness
	2	2	4.5.B	Readiness
	3	3	4.5.D	Readiness
	4	3	4.6.D	Readiness
	5	2	4.4.A	Readiness
	6	2	4.3.E	Readiness
	7	1	4.2.H	Supporting
	8	1	4.2.C	Supporting
	9	1	4.3.C	Supporting
	10	2	4.4.H	Readiness
Practice Exercise 23	1	2	4.5.A	Readiness
	2	3	4.7.D	Supporting
	3	2	4.4.A	Readiness
	4	4	4.10.E	Supporting
	5	4	4.9.B	Supporting
	6	3	4.6.D	Readiness
	7	4	4.9.A	Readiness
	8	1	4.2.G	Readiness
	9	1	4.3.D	Readiness
	10	2	4.4.H	Readiness
Practice Exercise 24	1	2	4.3.E	Readiness
	2	2	4.5.B	Readiness
	3	1	4.3.A	Supporting
	4	1	4.2.F	Supporting
	5	2	4.5.A	Readiness
	6	1	4.2.B	Readiness
	7	3	4.8.C	Readiness
	8	3	4.6.B	Supporting
	9	2	4.4.E	Supporting
	10	3	4.7.C	Readiness
Practice Exercise 25	1	2	4.4.H	Readiness
	2	1	4.2.G	Readiness
	3	4	4.9.A	Readiness
	4	4	4.10.A	Supporting
	5	1	4.4.A	Readiness
	6	3	4.5.D	Readiness
	7	2	4.4.G	Supporting
	8	2	4.4.A	Readiness
	9	2	4.5.B	Readiness
	10	2	4.4.G	Supporting

Top Tips: Preparing for Today's Tests

Ways to Build Mathematical Thinking at Home

	TIME Time with adults is the first step! Checking in for a few minutes as your child works on homework will give you a great idea of what is going on at school.
	IDEAS Ask your child's teacher what the four or five "big ideas" of the year will be in math so you know what to support at home.
	MULTI-STEP and MULTI-ANSWER Be aware that many of today's word problems have multiple steps and sometimes more than one correct answer.
	ENVIRONMENT Set up a quiet place for at-home study where your child can concentrate without distractions.
	FIND As a family, find examples of math in the news, such as temperature changes. Having your child compare these numbers shows real-life applications of math.
	OPPORTUNITIES Make opportunities for using math at home, such as doubling recipes, making change, balancing a checkbook, and reading a clock.
	REVIEW Review by using specific prompts such as, "Name the most challenging problem you did in math this week." Or, "What is your favorite math tool to use?"
	KEEP Keep a positive math outlook! Instead of commenting, "I was never any good at math," assure your child that even if math is challenging, there are supports available at home and at school.
	INTERNET The Internet has many free and engaging math games. Just ten minutes of practice per day can help reinforce skills and yield long-term results.
	DIRECTIONS Having your child repeat directions in their own words is a clarifying activity when approaching a math task.
	SHARE Share with your child how you used math during your day to solidify its importance.

Top Tips: Preparing for Today's Tests *(cont.)*

Ways to Succeed During Mathematical Tests

	THINK Think about what the problem is saying and asking you to do.
	INFORMATION Carefully examine the information given in the problem, such as numbers, graphs, and/or charts.
	MULTI-STEP and MULTI-ANSWER Many word problems have several steps, and more than one answer may be correct.
	ELIMINATE Eliminate any multiple-choice responses that you know cannot be correct based on logical reasoning.
	FIX Fixing and adjusting your thinking is a part of math. If a problem-solving approach does not work, learn from it, and try again.
	OPERATIONS Choose the best operation to solve the problem. Prove your work with words, numbers, and/or pictures.
	READ Read and re-read carefully to be sure you understand the task. Read and re-read your own work to be sure it is complete and makes sense.
	KEEP IT POSITIVE Keep a positive math outlook! When facing a math challenge, perhaps you can do part of the problem, if not the entire problem. Or maybe you can skip a part for now and come back to it later. A positive attitude helps you work through solutions that do not come quickly.
	I DON'T GET IT "I don't get it" is NOT a question! Ask specific questions about specific parts of a math challenge in class, and ask about directions you do not understand.
	DIRECTIONS Directions are there for a reason. Read them carefully, and check each one off as you complete it.
	STRATEGIES You know them; now use them! Use strategies such as work backward, guess and check, make a table/chart/list, and draw a picture to help solve problems.

Mathematics Tools

LENGTH

Customary

1 mile (mi) = 1,760 yards (yd)
1 yard (yd) = 3 feet (ft)
1 foot (ft) = 12 inches (in.)

Metric

1 kilometer (km) = 1,000 meters (m)
1 meter (m) = 100 centimeters (cm)
1 centimeter (cm) = 10 millimeters (mm)

VOLUME AND CAPACITY

Customary

1 gallon (gal) = 4 quarts (qt)
1 quart (qt) = 2 pints (pt)
1 pint (pt) = 2 cups (c)
1 cup (c) = 8 fluid ounces (fl oz)

Metric

1 liter (L) = 1,000 milliliters (mL)

WEIGHT AND MASS

Customary

1 ton (T) = 2,000 pounds(lb)
1 pound = 16 ounces (oz)

Metric

1 kilogram (kg) = 1,000 grams (g)
1 gram (g) = 1,000 milligrams (mg)

TIME

1 year = 12 months
1 year = 52 weeks
1 week = 7 days
1 day = 24 hours
1 hour = 60 minutes
1 minute = 60 seconds

PERIMETER

Square $\qquad$ $P = 4s$
Rectangle $\quad P = l + w + l + w$ or $P = 2l + 2w$

AREA

Square $\qquad$ $A = s \times s$
Rectangle $\qquad$ $A = l \times w$

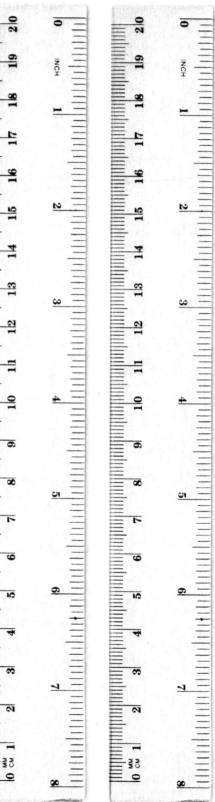

Answer Key

Practice Exercise 1 (pages 11–14)

1. D
2. H
3. B
4. H
5. B
6. G
7. A
8. H
9. D
10. 224

Practice Exercise 2 (pages 15–18)

1. C
2. J
3. A
4. F
5. C
6. J
7. C
8. G
9. A
10. 128

Practice Exercise 3 (pages 19–22)

1. B
2. J
3. C
4. G
5. A
6. G
7. D
8. H
9. C
10. 307.3

Practice Exercise 4 (pages 23–26)

1. C
2. G
3. C
4. J
5. D
6. G
7. C
8. G
9. A
10. 107

Practice Exercise 5 (pages 27–30)

1. C
2. G
3. C
4. G
5. D
6. G
7. C
8. H
9. D
10. 178

Practice Exercise 6 (pages 31–34)

1. C
2. G
3. B
4. J
5. A
6. H
7. D
8. H
9. A
10. 517

Answer Key *(cont.)*

Appendix F

Practice Exercise 7 (pages 35–38)

1. D
2. F
3. C
4. G
5. D
6. H
7. B
8. J
9. B
10. 96.98

Practice Exercise 8 (pages 39–42)

1. B
2. G
3. C
4. H
5. D
6. H
7. D
8. H
9. C
10. 336

Practice Exercise 9 (pages 43–46)

1. C
2. J
3. B
4. F
5. B
6. G
7. C
8. F
9. D
10. 10

Practice Exercise 10 (pages 47–50)

1. B
2. H
3. C
4. J
5. B
6. F
7. C
8. G
9. D
10. 270.96

Practice Exercise 11 (pages 51–54)

1. A
2. G
3. C
4. J
5. C
6. G
7. C
8. G
9. A
10. 121

Practice Exercise 12 (pages 55–58)

1. A
2. H
3. B
4. J
5. B
6. G
7. B
8. J
9. B
10. 5.5

Answer Key (cont.)

Practice Exercise 13 (pages 59–62)

1. D
2. H
3. A
4. G
5. D
6. J
7. A
8. H
9. B
10. 800

Practice Exercise 14 (pages 63–66)

1. B
2. J
3. A
4. J
5. B
6. F
7. A
8. H
9. A
10. 20

Practice Exercise 15 (pages 67–70)

1. D
2. G
3. C
4. H
5. C
6. J
7. A
8. H
9. B
10. 130°

Practice Exercise 16 (pages 71–74)

1. C
2. G
3. A
4. H
5. B
6. J
7. B
8. H
9. B
10. 87

Practice Exercise 17 (pages 75–78)

1. B
2. H
3. D
4. F
5. D
6. G
7. C
8. G
9. A
10. 19.8

Practice Exercise 18 (pages 79–82)

1. B
2. F
3. C
4. F
5. D
6. J
7. D
8. J
9. D
10. 450

Answer Key *(cont.)*

Practice Exercise 19 (pages 83–86)

1. A
2. F
3. D
4. G
5. D
6. G
7. A
8. F
9. D
10. 980

Practice Exercise 20 (pages 87–90)

1. D
2. G
3. B
4. F
5. D
6. H
7. B
8. H
9. B
10. 34.17

Practice Exercise 21 (pages 91–94)

1. C
2. F
3. B
4. F
5. D
6. H
7. B
8. G
9. D
10. 90

Practice Exercise 22 (pages 95–98)

1. D
2. G
3. C
4. G
5. A
6. J
7. C
8. J
9. C
10. 12

Practice Exercise 23 (pages 99–102)

1. C
2. J
3. A
4. G
5. D
6. H
7. B
8. F
9. B
10. 378

Practice Exercise 24 (pages 103–106)

1. D
2. H
3. C
4. G
5. C
6. G
7. D
8. H
9. B
10. 150°

Answer Key (cont.)

Practice Exercise 25 (pages 107–110)

1. A
2. G
3. C
4. F
5. D
6. H
7. D
8. G
9. C
10. 370

51703—*Time For Kids: Practicing for STAAR Success*

Notes

Notes